WEST
TO THE DAWN

WEST
TO THE DAWN

*An American Woman's
Adventures in Thailand Heal
Her Wounded Soul*

*To Jennie and Tristan —
With happy memories
Jackie McKinley
June 2007*

Jackie McKinley

To order additional copies of this book, contact:
Xlibris Corporation
1-888-795-4274
www.Xlibris.com
Orders@Xlibris.com
16334

CONTENTS

Dedication
To
Lorie
Mark
and
John

With all my love

To my friends and family who will read this book—

I offer you my sincere gratitude for your love and support over the years. I have been exceedingly blessed by all of you.

I am especially grateful to my children, Lorie and Mark. They encouraged me to go to Thailand, then wrote me a letter every week for two years, plus taking time to come and visit me.

My thanks to my sister, Betty Jensen, and my friend, Molly Saunders, for their faithful letters, sending me needed supplies, and handling countless reports and letters to church, school, family, and friends.

My writing group encouraged my writing efforts, then challenged me to tell the truth and the whole story. Thank you, Jill Plummer, for the hours we spent together, rewriting and polishing my manuscript. Finally, thanks to Carol Markos who did the final proofreading.

I'm grateful to those who read my manuscript, gave helpful suggestions and corrected data: Ruth Cadwallader, Ed Hudspith, Jo-an and Art Larson, Elaine Lewis, Dot Turnbull and Mary Weideman.

Then there is my husband, John, who made me write. His patience, understanding, and support are responsible for the completion of my story.

Thank you all,

Jackie McKinley

FLYING INTO MY DREAM

The fierce tropical storm outside the plane window reflected my feelings as we traveled toward Bangkok Don Muan Airport. While rain lashed the side of the 727 and the pilot struggled against buffeting winds, I too fought a storm within myself. When the plane landed I would be committed. There would be no turning back.

My whole life seemed to have led me to this hour and to this country of Thailand, and as the plane continued to buck and challenge the wind, thoughts of my childhood crowded in. I sensed Mother sitting beside me, her knitting in her lap, needles flying, eager and excited about the events ahead. She was probably the person most responsible for my being here. Even though she had spent her whole life in a small midwestern farming community caring for her husband and five children, she had always pursued a strong interest in world affairs. Whenever anyone of note came to town to visit or speak, they inevitably ended up sitting around our crowded old oak dining table, enjoying Mother's savory German cooking.

I recalled sitting on the floor in our tiny living room, listening attentively to one of these visitors—a small, plain, compact woman with faded gray hair pulled tightly into a round bun at the nape of her neck. She was a missionary recently returned from central China and she told tales of children who lived in simple mud huts and walked miles each day in rain or snow just to learn how to read. She described plagues and floods where millions died. Her stories of Chinese festivals enthralled me: colorful dancing dragons, firecrackers, boisterous plays performed in the market square. It was she and others like her who sowed in me my love for Asia.

Later there had been the Broadway show, "Anna and the King of Siam." Anna, in 1879, had sailed up the Chao Phya River to Bangkok on her way to becoming a teacher for the children of the Royal Court. She had traveled to meet the King. Now I was here to meet the people.

I watched the flight attendants move gingerly down the aisle attempting to serve drinks while the plane continued to roll and roar through the menacing sky. Sunny Singapore was left far behind. Here it was dark and threatening. I shivered.

The determining reason for my being on this plane was the sudden death, four years before, of my husband, Lee. I tried to push painful images and disturbing thoughts away but they insisted on coming. I wanted Lee to be sitting here with me enjoying an experience we had dreamed about for twenty-two years: ever since we had sat in the bleachers of the Cow Palace in San Francisco, listening to President-elect John F. Kennedy introduce his plans for the Peace Corps. Driving home we talked enthusiastically about volunteering our teaching skills for this kind of program. We were eager to take off right then! But we had two small children. Such plans must wait.

During our twenty-eight year marriage Lee had several bouts of severe illness. Then, suddenly, at the age of fifty-eight he was gone. To lose my husband was the most devastating experience of my life. No one could have prepared me for it. I was angry and bitter. Four years later I was still in pain.

Even today I find it difficult to use the word "suicide". The word brings back vivid memories and pain. When people ask I just say "Lee died." When some have pushed and asked "how" and I do say suicide—we are both uncomfortable.

Now those memories of his five-year depression and his final weeks of suffering, return. All those hours talking with counselors, therapists, psychiatrists, ministers, and friends, yet I could see he was only getting worse. On Thursday after school I went to see his most recent counselor, hiding my appointment from Lee under the pretext of a late meeting.

He was in "group therapy" at the time which was painful as the group seemed to be saying, "You've got everything to live for. Just get with it." I had gotten so I even hesitated to ask him about his sessions because they were so upsetting, but he felt this was an important kind of therapy he hadn't tried.

Earlier in the week we had spent the evening talking with a friend who had written a book on depression, and the friend and I both tried to get Lee to talk about his feelings and where he was coming from. When I pressed him again on the drive home, he would only say, "I'm fine. What are you worried about?"—a typical Lee answer. I could never get more out of him.

So that Thursday afternoon I told the counselor I was desperately afraid my husband was going to take his life and I didn't know how to stop him. Should I stay home? Should I be with him 24 hours a day to keep him from doing it? The counselor said, "If he is going to take his life, he will find a way, whether you are there or not."

Next morning when I awoke, the questions haunted me: Should I call for a substitute? Should I stay home? How could I make Lee share what he was really feeling? He never had in the past. How real were my fears? He had never talked about suicide. Was it my imagination?

Lee awoke and struggled out of bed complaining of weariness. Since he was on a leave of absence from teaching, I

encouraged him to go back to sleep and enjoy a relaxed Friday
saying that when I came home we would plan something fun for
the weekend.

Mark, our son, was graduating from college in three weeks
and as I drove to school I prayed over and over, "Hold on Lee! The
school year is almost over. We'll find hope and help this summer."

Once I entered the classroom with 28 eager fourth graders I
didn't have much time to think about myself. Therefore it wasn't
until I was driving home after school that my anxiety returned.
Why was I so fearful? Other people committed suicide—not my
husband. I was being overly anxious. Of course he'll be fine.

But when I pulled up to the house and unlocked the front
door—I was afraid. Somehow I knew. I didn't want to look down
that hall to our bedroom door. It was closed. Now I was sure. Heart
pounding, I slowly approached and cautiously opened it. Lee lay
in bed looking very natural. My worst fears were realized.

I glanced at my watch. The plane droned on through the night.
I felt suspended in time, in a dark cocoon that shut out everything
around me. Thoughts of the past and anxiety for the future tumbled
in my mind.

"May I take your tray?" The flight attendant's voice pulled me
back to the present.

After Lee was gone I had kept busy trying to shut out the hurt
and loneliness. Although the pain did not go away, it did hide and
allow me to function. I taught school and volunteered for even
more projects. My two children were grown and away from home
so, trying to create some semblance of family, I rented their rooms
to college students.

After three years I became aware that I was changing into
someone I didn't like. I felt sorry for myself and became angry
easily, finding fault with friends and fellow workers. I realized I
must do something, but just changing my daily life didn't help. I
needed to turn things around, but how?

All during my childhood my German mother had told me,
"You can't run away from problems. You face them. Deal with

them. Keep a stiff upper lip—and never give up!" However, in my contemplative reading, I read of many who **did** "run away" from society and daily routine for a needed time of quiet; a time to reflect and pull back. Gradually this idea began to appeal to me. The thought of a pilgrimage, a journey to restore my soul . . . became my quest.

The idea of the Peace Corps or overseas volunteer service, my childhood dream, the dream I had shared with Lee, returned. Would traveling to a different country, a different culture, a place where I knew no one, be the answer? But how to do this? I was in my early fifties, had a steady teaching job, a large home to maintain, and no extra financial resources. The idea kept nagging at me, and I began to explore opportunities.

Plans started to fall into place. Friends in real estate assured me I could rent my home. My children encouraged me. I found a program sponsored by my Presbyterian church called Volunteer in Mission. It was similar to the Peace Corps in that you are a volunteer English teacher for a two-year assignment, and I applied to both of these organizations.

I filled out tedious forms, took medical tests, and mailed recommendations. Then I waited. Timing was crucial as I had to juggle teaching, rental of my house, and packing, with dates for departure. It seemed to take forever.

One February morning while I was at work the call came. The message said, "We have a request from Thailand for you to teach at Dara Academy in Chiang Mai. Are you interested?"

Was I interested? I would have left the next day if possible.

*   *   *

News of my acceptance as a Volunteer in Mission spread quickly and I was delighted when my Presbyterian Session voted to pay my air fare as I would have no salary for two years. Room and board would be provided by the Thais.

At the farewell service planned by my church, I felt a trace of discomfort when several said, "We are so proud of you." I knew I was going for purely selfish reasons. I was running away. My primary motive was not to help others but to help myself. I was off on a personal pilgrimage.

My second deception with my friends and my church related to the fact that I was to be a "Volunteer in Mission," which qualified me to have my name entered as a missionary in the Mission Yearbook, and I was not comfortable with this. Many people still looked upon missionaries as people who went overseas to "save the heathen." I had no intention of trying to change people's religion or way of life. I was to be an English teacher making an effort to help those in a developing country improve their standard of living and become major participants in the international community. When asked why I was going, I never mentioned the word "missionary" but always called myself a teacher.

*   *   *

Jumbled thoughts of my mother, Anna, childhood experiences, Lee and our shattered dreams, receded as seat belts clicked shut, and seat backs were pulled upright. The weary flight attendants made one last trip down the aisle as the pilot instructed them to take their seats. The storm had calmed. I was ready to land.

TAGGING ALONG
IN BANGKOK

My arrival in Bangkok was unsettling. Since I was not a seasoned traveler, I was apprehensive about going through customs on my own and tucked myself in behind a young couple to follow the crowds.

I did look forward to seeing my friends, Ruth and Bill, former schoolmates from California who now worked with the American Friends Service Committee (AFSC) and with the United Nations Refugee program in Thailand. I had thought of their presence as being one of the real pluses of my being assigned here.

As soon as I reached a point where I could see the people who waited to greet passengers, I searched for familiar faces. No Ruth and Bill. They must be there somewhere! But, no, and I did not find them when I had finished customs. Hearing rain pelting down outside the building, I told myself traffic must have held them up and sat down on a bench to wait.

After an hour of growing increasingly anxious I cautiously approached a telephone. The Thai directions on the black box, and lack of Thai money, left me floundering. "Can I help?" A young Thai gentleman had seen my distress. When I told him of my dilemma, he contributed the necessary coins and dialed my friend's number. I hope he knew how grateful I was for that moment of kindness, but he was gone before I could thank him. At the other end of the line, a Thai voice answered. It was the cook, and we had an incredible conversation as we tried to communicate with my bit of Thai and her broken English. When I hung up I hoped I was right in understanding that Ruth and Bill were on their way to the airport. Again I settled down to wait.

I was greatly relieved when, a short time later, I saw two familiar figures approaching and ran to greet them. Evidently there had been confusion about my time of arrival. I wondered if this mix-up was a forecast of my life in Thailand.

How fortunate I was to be taken to Ruth and Bill's small but very comfortable home off a narrow alley in the central part of Bangkok. Ruth had filled each corner with beautiful Thai crafts which I would later admire, but now I was anxious to find and enjoy their guest room and a comfortable bed!

A good night's sleep performed wonders, and I was up early the next morning, persuading Bill to plug my electric typewriter into an adapter so I could record my trip. I was now in a country that used 220 voltage instead of 120. I must remember to adapt all the electrical appliances I had brought with me. My electric typewriter weighed about forty pounds and had cost me an enormous sum to transport to Thailand. It was also an added burden to cart along with my two large suitcases, each filled with supplies I had been told to bring for the next two years! I often wondered if carrying that typewriter halfway around the world had been a wise decision but I could not do without my faithful tool.

By 8:30 a.m. I was dripping wet. In the mirror I saw that my face had turned beet red and I quickly exchanged a wash cloth for the kleenex I used to mop my brow. This was my first time in a semi-tropical climate and I thanked my lucky stars I had been assigned to Chiang Mai in the North, the coolest place in Thailand. I soon discovered I did not have the right clothes for Bangkok. Around the house Ruth wore only a shift with spaghetti straps but I had brought jeans and T-shirts, which were hot! Hair which had looked great when I got up was "fizzing" fast. Damp curls stuck to my forehead creating the semblance of a very disheveled lady.

Ruth interrupted my typing to announce she had to go into the main part of Bangkok for a meeting. "I'd love to tag along," I said, "and then I'll head off to see the sights." She seemed a bit disconcerted and tried to discourage me. I confidently assured her that my favorite pastime in a foreign city was to roam around on my own. "I did it in Singapore, I can do it here." I changed my clothes and soon we were on a bus headed toward town.

I discovered that Bangkok was different from any other place I had been. My stopover in an easy-to-navigate Singapore had been very misleading. The city was clean. They had English street signs and I could imagine I was in London or New York with its elegant shops, wide mosaic sidewalks, and attractive displays.

Bangkok was like a maze. Very new and ancient houses, shops and small industries, stood alongside burdened sidewalks littered with boxes, trash, and carts. The noise was deafening as honking trucks, taxis, and golf-cart type vehicles called tuk-tuks all hurried in different directions. Fumes rose to greet each breath. I coughed and dodged bicycles.

When I left Ruth at her meeting, she carefully pointed me toward my first destination, the Oriental Hotel. One of the most expensive and elegant in the world, it sits on the edge of Thailand's largest river, the Chao Phya running through the center of Bangkok. After exploring the luxurious public rooms and gardens, I asked a few questions of the many English-speaking people in the lobby and then confidently took a river taxi across the Chao Phya. I was eager to visit Wat Arun, the Temple of the Dawn, seen by all river travelers. It stands majestically at the edge of the river—it's awesome glow the result of thousands of pieces of Chinese porcelain embedded in cement walls.

My first wat! How exciting to finally visit a place I had read about back in California. I had learned that a wat is a Buddhist temple used for worship and teaching, and Wat Arun was one of the tallest religious structures in Thailand. I slowly climbed the steep steps of the tower, stopping often to use the wash cloth I had wisely put in my bag. Reaching the top I had a magnificent view of the temple compound. Across the river lay the city of Bangkok.

Returning to the base of the temple, I watched Buddhists of all ages bringing offerings of food and flowers. I was amazed at the many Buddha statues covered with gold leaf, and tried to understand the meaning of the colorful murals that lined so many walls.

Confidently I caught a river taxi to visit Wat Po. My guide book told me that this was the oldest and largest Buddhist temple in Bangkok and it was enormous, its size rendering it impossible for me to see all of the buildings, pavilions, statues and gardens in one day. I was especially interested in the many chedis—tiered, spire-like pagodas containing ancient relics. The seventy-one small chedis contained the ashes of royal descendants, while the twenty larger ones held relics of the Buddha. These sacred mementos might be fingernail clippings, hairs, or bits of clothing. My camera was busy capturing unusual structures, gold-leafed statues, and buildings covered in mosaic tiles.

Beautiful Wat Po

I wandered outside the temple to observe Thai women selling foodstuffs on the sidewalks, their small booths or simple mats nestled close against the wall. They all seemed happy, while talking and visiting. I noticed them eating each other's wares but saw no baht, the Thai money, being exchanged. Since I had been cautioned about eating food sold on the streets, I had to satisfy myself with looking and smelling! The various sliced fruits were especially tempting until I noticed all the flies. Small pieces of meat sizzled over hot coals—I breathed in the delicious smell of street-side barbecues. Brightly colored jelly shapes laid out on trays looked delicious and tempting, but I resisted until learning which Thai food was safe for me.

I had walked miles—time to head for home. I spent thirty minutes trying to find the number 8 bus which would take me back to Ruth's street. I was far from the big hotels and no one in this area seemed to understand my English. After being given contradictory directions several times, I eventually arrived in a large square with many buses. A quick search yielded an ancient looking vehicle with a number 8! I heaved a sigh of relief and climbed aboard.

As we took off down the street, I looked out the window and checked my Bangkok map, trying to locate familiar street signs or monuments. An hour passed and then thoroughly confused and convinced I was on the wrong bus I got off. What to do? I was far from the crowded area of the main city and surrounded by small shops and houses. My attempts to talk with people received smiles, giggles and shaking heads. "Do you speak English?" No luck. My heart lept when I saw some school girls in uniforms, and thinking they must certainly learn English in school I asked them my question. All I received were more giggles.

Tired, hungry and frustrated, I leaned against a wall. Suddenly I remembered the address card Ruth had given me, English on one side and Thai on the other. I pulled it from my bag and soon found a taxi. The driver nodded when I showed him the card. Nervously I prayed the whole way home to Ruth's that I was actually being taken to my desired destination.

It took a half hour and when I entered the house I found my hosts worrying about me as it was getting late. After I described my adventure on the bus, they decided I had taken a small numeral 8 instead of a large numeral 8. They also congratulated me on having managed so well. In weary retrospect, I had thoroughly enjoyed my first of many fascinating days in Bangkok and yet . . .

> *I'm finally here in this place I've chosen to help rid me of this awful guilt. I don't feel whole any more. How can I lead a normal life—face people—having caused his death. My love— our marriage—why wasn't it enough?*
>
> *So many loved and admired him. Even his high school students voted him favorite teacher. Twenty-eight married years. I've gone over all of it a million times. Where did I go wrong? So many places.*

Why couldn't we communicate better? Was it all my fault? Didn't I care enough? I know I was impatient at times, took over and made too many decisions. Did I give him a chance to express his opinion?

But it was hard. He'd been so sick. All that rheumatoid arthritis at the beginning of our marriage. I remember that Christmas vacation when his doctor told him to try to stop taking cortisone for it was only "covering up" his infection. Since he had two weeks off from teaching, this would be a good time to try.

The arthritis had been getting worse. I was scared when he dropped me off each morning at my school and drove on alone to his teaching job several miles away. He had to manually lift his left leg to put it on the brake. I always packed him a lunch as his classroom was on the third floor of the Jr-Hi School where he taught, and it was so painful to climb those stairs he would stay up there all day.

Lee hadn't taken his pills that last Friday morning before our holiday—AND—instead of a two week recovery period, he didn't get out of bed for over 60 days. It was six months before the fever and infection subsided.

That was a shock. It was a year and a half before he was able to return to teaching. During that time, I managed our home, taught school, took care of his medical needs and generally had complete responsibility for all day to day decisions.

When Lee was able to return to work, the pattern was set, and I remained primarily in charge. This was NOT good. But we had such good years after the children were born. He enjoyed his family—our many trips across the country—our summer in Washington D.C. while he studied at Georgetown University— our camping vacations—his success as a teacher. He even wrote a social studies textbook for his school district.

Where did the depression and suicide come from? The agonizing question twisted in my heart as I tossed and turned.

Oh, God, please let me find the answer here.

HEARTBREAK AND DISBELIEF

During that visit in July of 1982, Ruth and Bill, who were working with refugees for the United Nations, took me to see two camps in Northern Thailand.

At this time the problem of the Laotian refugees was enormous. Although Laos had a long tradition of benevolent monarchy, strong Chinese and Vietnamese influences had caused many of the people to embrace quasi-socialist, if not Communist, government. Under Prince Souphanau, Laos became a divided country and what had been an easy-going, unrestricted society became rigid and tightly controlled. Many of the tribal people, including the Hmong, Yao and Lowland Lao, who had emigrated earlier from China, now became extremely discontented, and when the problems were further exacerbated by the CIA using Laos as a base for the war in Vietnam, many citizens abandoned everything and fled.

Now agencies from around the world were in Thailand, working to solve the problem of what to do with these destitute people. My friends, knowing of my interest, had applied to the

Minister of Interior for permission for me to enter the camps with them. This was a rare privilege for a tourist at that time and I was enormously grateful.

Heartbreaking and unbelievable are the two words that come to mind when I think of my two days visiting Sobtuang and Ban Nam Yao refugee camps. These were both near the Laos border in northeast Thailand, about an hour's drive outside the city of Nan.

The first day was especially exciting as I bounced along in the back of a pickup truck, up, down and around those lush green hills, on semi-graveled roads through some of the most beautiful country I had seen in Asia. We careened past water buffalo pulling creaking wooden carts, and villagers with hoes over their shoulders, heading for work in the rice fields. Dogs, cats and pigs lay stretched out on the edges of the roads, napping in the sun. Chickens barely escaped our wheels.

We passed through several small Thai villages, made colorful by golden-orange corn which hung in rows under the houses to dry. All of these homes were built on stilts, with the living area a platform eight to ten feet off the ground. The walls were made of bamboo, and I couldn't help thinking that the thinly thatched roofs must provide scant protection from winter rains. Away from the villages, dense foliage lined the road, and through it I could see plodding water buffalo pulling simple wooden plows in the now flooded dike-edged rice fields.

In the distance a lush forest of teak trees crowned the hills. In contrast to all this beauty, dust from the road covered our faces and clothes in suffocating grit. Sobtuang and Ban Nam Yao were a considerable distance apart, both located in isolated areas on mountain slopes. It was an incredible sight to round that last curve in the road and see the refugee camp shacks, crawling up and down steep mountainsides like a child's wooden blocks, ready for play. These tribal people liked to live close together, so they built their houses almost touching.

Three different Laotian tribes, the Hmong, Yao, and Htin, lived in these two camps, a total of nine to ten thousand people crowded together. Many had been here for six or seven years, some transferred three or four times. They lived in continual uncertainty. For instance, the people in the Sobtuang Camp had been told they would all be moved to Ban Nam Yao by the end of August. But they had been told regularly over the years that they would be moved, or their camp closed, so now they believed nothing until it happened. When we visited the Ban Nam Yao camp the next day, there was no evidence that the housing for these people had even begun. I wondered how I would live with these uncertainties in my life. Would I be willing to learn a trade, cultivate the earth, begin schooling, if every week or so I was told that my stay was limited?

At this time, a big effort was being made to "repatriate" the refugees and convince them to return home under UN protection. Many of the international workers felt that this might be the best solution. However, in both camps were many people who had "cooperated" with our CIA years before in Laos, in exchange for money and rice. These same people were no longer welcome in their own country, and although guaranteed UN protection, many were not convinced they would be safe.

The problem was complicated by the fact that these camps sometimes earned their nickname, "Fool's Paradise." Many inhabitants had been there for seven years, had been taken care of, provided with food and housing. It was a beautiful, comfortable area in which to live. So, why leave?

International workers from many organizations worked here and the majority impressed me with their dedication and philosophy. They seemed eager to have the refugees return to their homes, knowing their skills and support were needed there. Success would mean that the international teams had worked themselves out of their jobs, and though most were willing to do this, some, I thought, were not.

While at the camps I also saw evidence of how these organizations were trying to involve the tribal people in crafts and industries indigenous to their culture and country. Their aim was to promote self-sufficiency; if a woman wanted to learn how to weave, a counselor started by teaching her husband how to make the simple machines necessary for her work. This made it a family project.

As I walked around the compound I observed many practicing new skills. Women struggled to understand the workings of a sewing machine. Some men listened to instructions on how to make water jugs, while others carefully handled hot molten iron in a forge. A large number worked on intricate silver and bronze jewelry and ultimately these tribal handicrafts provided the main income for both camps.

On the second day we visited the Tom Dooley Heritage Hospital at Ban Nam Yao. I had previously read of Tom Dooley's amazing work with these refugees and how he was one of the first to become aware of their plight and need for medical care, thus providing the impetus for many projects that followed. Because the most serious problems at the hospital were diarrhea and malaria, a major effort was being made to educate tribal folk about cleanliness and preventative health measures. I was impressed with the training books filled with pictures and simple easily understood instructions that had been developed by the American Friends Service Committee.

I listened to AFSC personnel speak to camp leaders. "Your children are your most important resource. They are important for your future. You must teach the women to read and write so they can help the children."

The Hmong leader of the camp replied, "In our tribe in Laos, the women were of no importance. Now with your organization here you are teaching us the opposite. We will try." I wondered if this could really be done since I saw only men in positions of leadership at either camp.

We walked for miles up and down steep dirt trails, with Ruth stopping often to visit with people willing to talk. We spent hours listening to their stories. Since I could not communicate in any of their languages, I watched faces, trying to discover what these people were feeling. I did not see many smiles or hear laughter or singing but I didn't see sadness either, so I finally decided that what I saw was resignation. "This is where we are—this is what we must do— just exist and make the best of it."

We were invited to have lunch in the home of one of the refugees. Gingerly I climbed the steep pole ladder up into the house. As we sat with the men on the rough wooden floor in the front of the single room, I could hear the women preparing food in the rear. The kitchen consisted of a small platform extending out from the main room. I was told all cooking was done here so that in case of fire, only this part of the home would be damaged and simply fall to the ground.

We were each furnished with a tin spoon, and food was served on a dented tin plate. I was quietly warned not to drink any of the water, but did enjoy sticky rice, noodles, pork, and cucumbers. When I expressed my amazement that they could feed us so well, I was informed that one of the people in our party had purchased the food ahead of time, and taken it for the family to prepare. I was embarrassed to eat such fine food and would have preferred to eat what the villagers normally ate. The women who had prepared our food did not join us at the meal, but sat quietly in the back of the room. I left feeling disturbed and overwhelmed by the inequities of life.

During our walk, I especially kept my eye on the children. Being a mother and a teacher, I could not help but wonder about their lives. One small boy, probably seven or eight years old, had just returned from spending a few hours in the makeshift school, and let me look at his notebook. The writing was simple and crudely done. Unfortunately, few children were encouraged to attend the classes set up by the international community. Most preferred to spend their time playing under houses, or on small flat dirt areas with sticks or stones. I saw no evidence of any athletic equipment. No balls. No bats. No toys. A number of young girls sat giggling under a tree. The first signs of happiness I had seen that day.

Jackie checking homework

Wherever we walked, I was aware of the distant barbed wire fence surrounding the camp—a fence that really didn't mean much as in many places it was held up only by a stick. I looked across the mountains to Laos. There was only thick jungle between this camp and the refugees' homeland. Just a short walk, but what awaited at the end of the trail?

The problems I observed that day did seem insurmountable and I left with a feeling of great admiration for the job being done by the international organizations. I also pondered the role of the United States in this situation. It was hard to picture these people, in their colorful tribal dress, on American streets.

The whole time I was in the camps I was trying to imagine myself in the place of the women I saw. How would I adjust if torn from my home and community? Would I be bitter and angry at the world if I had to live in a detention center and my life was controlled by others? How much effort would I put into improving my circumstances, trying to learn new skills under adverse conditions, with no guarantee that I would ever leave the camp? Watching the children was the saddest part. I thought of my own son and daughter and the advantages they had compared to camp children living in meager conditions on a remote mountain side. What incentive was there for them to learn, to study, to improve?

The hopelessness of their situation brought back thoughts of Lee and the things he told me about his childhood. His father was an important minister in the American Baptist Denomination pastoring in some of its largest churches and teaching in one of its seminaries. He was Convention President and later responsible for its mission program in Asia which involved a lot of travel.

I remember once at the dinner table in our home, he seemed to be bragging when he told how he was so dedicated to his work that only once did he have time to take his children to a circus. That night in bed Lee said that single day was one of the highlights of his childhood. He could not recall any other events apart from church functions that he had attended with his father.

Lee also spoke often of difficulties in school. Once he was promoted because the class was too big and it had been a terrible strain to be with the "big kids" and fall behind in his studies. Then, when he was finally making headway and feeling good about learning, his father took a job as minister of a large church in another state, deciding to start the job in May, even though the children wanted to finish out the school year where they were. Again, the strain of starting a new school at the end of the school year caused Lee much anxiety and when as an adult, frustrated by significant reading problems, he had to spend many hours in classes to improve this skill, he blamed these two situations. Of course reading was the basic tool for his profession of history teacher.

During a Christmas vacation with my family, Lee told me how impressed he was when he saw my mother and father holding hands as they sat on the couch watching grandchildren opening their presents. He added that he had never seen his parents hug, kiss or even hold hands in his entire life.

He recalled when he was two or three years old, putting his small arms around his mother's legs and hugging her. "My, you're an affectionate child, aren't you?" she responded. He didn't do it again.

Because of all this, when our children were born Lee made a big effort to be an affectionate father. He did a good job of it, but it was not a natural reaction. Was the lack of attention and affection during his childhood part of his problem?

So, how would these children survive it all?

CITY OF CONTRASTS

"CITY OF ROSES." "MOST BEAUTIFUL WOMEN IN THE WORLD." "TEMPLE CITY." These were some of the things I had read about Chiang Mai, the second largest city in the country, and now, after three weeks of exploring Bangkok and visiting the refugee camps, I had waved goodbye to Ruth and Bill at the airport and following a short flight, was here.

I stepped off the small shuttle plane and was met by six people, their greeting so warm, I knew at once each would become a special friend. I relaxed as they took charge of my bags and whisked me away in their old Ford Wrangler to wind through city streets filled with busses, pedicabs, cars and trucks, all seeming in danger of imminent collision. I tried not to show my nervousness, breathing a secret sigh of relief when we made it safely to the home of Conrad and Carolyn, Presbyterian missionaries working at Payap University. This was my introduction to the weekly healthy Thai lunch they provided to supplement the diet of the volunteers, many of whom lived on small stipends, or with local families where meals were often meager. I thoroughly enjoyed the lively company and Thai

curries but was grateful when Ruth, my hostess, offered to take me
to where I would be staying until I could move into a place of my
own. Ruth was a widow from the States and I was told that for the
past ten years she had volunteered to teach piano to Thai students
at Payap University. The many awards won by her students were
an indication of her expert teaching skills.

Her home was not far away and I immediately loved the modest
teak floored house with its glassless windows which gave a feeling
of spaciousness despite the small rooms. Shown to my quarters, I
was glad to be left alone to relax. I hung up a few clothes then
stretched out on the bed. In no time I was fast asleep.

Dusk was falling when I awoke, refreshed and ready for my
promised introduction to the city. Ruth insisted we eat first. After
a light supper of sticky rice and honey baked chicken, we headed
for the Night Market, one of Chiang Mai's main attractions. It
was held in a large open space in the center of town, and was a
shopper's paradise, its amazing assortment of wares displayed on
tables, boxes, and boards.

I saw more Tribal people in their colorful jackets and black
trousers and admired the beautifully stitched articles they made
in their mountain villages. Never had I seen such intricate
workmanship!

I poured over all the typical Thai crafts. Silver jewelry and
bowls were laid out on bare boards, while bolts of Thai silk and
cotton lined up among shirts, dresses, and blouses. I loved the
unusual Celadon pottery and was amazed at the beauty of dishes
and sculptures fired to give a cracked appearance on their deep
green or brown glazing.

Carved teak, mostly elephant, but also water buffalo, lay on
simple mats on the ground along with candlestick holders, lamp
bases and many other items.

Black lacquerware of every imaginable size and shape delighted
me. It had been a favorite of mine since I had watched bamboo
strips being covered with layers of lacquer, then repeatedly polished
with ash and clay and painted with glowing, brilliant colors.

There was so much to see and smell and eat! Food vendors

filled every vacant space along the road, and the air quivered with the aroma of roasting meat, bananas, noodles, and Thai curries. No one would go hungry at this Night Market.

I watched and listened as my friends bargained over items they wished to purchase, but found myself getting more and more uncomfortable as they haggled over a few baht with people obviously in need. Finally I whispered my concern into Ruth's ear.

"It's all right," she said. "I used to feel that way, too, but really they don't expect you to pay what they ask. They've a set price they won't go under so they always make a profit. Don't worry, Jackie, you'll soon be doing it with the rest of us."

I felt better. Yes, I would learn to bargain, but I also knew I would always carry a feeling of guilt over some of my purchases. Later that night in bed, I ran through the events of the day and fell asleep filled with anticipation for the months to come.

It wasn't until I arrived in Chiang Mai that I was given my schedule and was disappointed to learn I was to teach fourth grade each morning in the International School and would only spend afternoons with Thai girls at Dara. Since my purpose in coming was to be involved with Thais and the Thai community this was depressing. But I promised myself I would get full-time work at Dara as soon as possible. Anyhow, I had a month before classes began and I was glad of this time to shop for my new home, learn how to use local transportation, and get to know this fascinating corner of the world.

City of Temples was not named in exaggeration. The first one I visited was on Doi Sutep, the mountain overlooking Chiang Mai. A two-bench mini bus, called a seelar, drove me up a twisty, narrow road and through many openings in the foliage, I had tempting glimpses of the city and plains below.

Legend has it that an especially holy relic was brought to Chiang Mai in 1371. To decide where it should be enshrined, it was placed on the back of an elephant, which promptly set out to climb the mountain. At the point where the great beast finally rested, the relic was buried and the first chedi built over it. The temple has been continually expanded and embellished ever since.

The colorful dragon serpents, or "naga", which line each side of the 209 steps up to the wat looked threatening but did not deter me from my climb to the top. When I finally arrived, the breathtaking view across Chiang Mai and the River Ping valley made the exhausting trip well worthwhile and I spent many minutes just looking.

Finally I entered the temple. It was one large space with walls of brightly painted murals depicting the previous lives of the Buddha, and cloisters filled with Buddhist statues. A glorious golden chedi arose from the center of the marble floor, and lacy golden umbrellas graced each corner. It was cool and peaceful and I found it hard to leave but I must—evening was coming.

In addition to wats on almost every corner of the city, the many saffron-swathed monks were an ever-present reminder that I was in a Buddhist country. I quickly learned that it was necessary to give up a front seat on the bus if one of them climbed on. Each morning I watched them pass the house on their rounds to collect food for the day. Ruth told me it was **not** begging, rather Thais thought that to give them food was both a privilege and a good way to earn merit for the afterlife.

It did not take me long to fall in love with this city of contrasts, but some things saddened me, such as the beggars who lined the bridge across the river. I was told some parents even made cripples out of their children, so people would feel pity and give them money. Many sidewalks were impassable because of broken concrete, and trash that was never removed. The air was often heavily polluted because of the thousands of motorcycles, cars, and buses and the burning of nearby fields. Moats were also polluted and foul-smelling.

It grieved me to see so many undernourished people, especially children who, at a tender age, worked in the market with their parents. Once, when I hired a pedicab driver to take me home from town, it started to rain, and the old gentleman began to cough and struggle as he peddled. I was torn with what to do. Since I could not insult him by getting out to walk, I suffered until reaching my door. I gave him an especially big tip, hoping he would go home and get out of the rain.

Chiang Mai was a mass of color. There were flower stalls which surpassed any I had seen in San Francisco. Dazzling poinsettia hedges stood ten to fifteen feet tall, competing with flaming double-headed bougainvilleas and hibiscus plants.

Beautiful women in flower market

Soon my month of relaxation was over and my apartment, located within a few blocks of each school was ready. It was simply an expanded bedroom on the second floor of an old mission house. It was small but had everything I needed. Its one square room measuring fifteen by fifteen feet had an enclosed bathroom and shower in one corner and a tiny kitchen along one wall. The only furniture was a bookcase with cupboard space and a single bed.

But what a thrill it was when I stepped out through beautiful teak double doors to find a large porch with floor-to-ceiling screens and a six-foot overhang to keep out the rain. Here there was another single bed, a table with four chairs, and a desk. Since this was the second floor of the house, it would be like living in a park, as my new home nestled among tall leafy trees. I looked forward with delight to eating, sleeping, and living "out-of-doors" for the next two years.

Other volunteers also rented mini-apartments on this second floor. One of them, Donna, arrived from Texas, and quickly agreed to share a maid with me. The young woman we hired was inexperienced as a cook, but managed basic chores well enough while also doing our laundry and shopping. Having our laundry done was rather essential as the only way to wash our clothes was a cement slab beyond the house with a cold water spigot. Chiang Mai had not yet succumbed to having laundromats in the town. The second problem was the ability to dry clothes outdoors on a clothesline in a country where it might rain two or three times a day with brilliant sunshine in between. While we were at our schools teaching, it was helpful to have someone take our clothes into our rooms and spread them over the furniture to dry.

Occasionally, when I had time, I liked to go to the food market which was located in a large building in the center of town and covered a whole block. At first I was shocked to see table after table of meat laid out on oilcloth while sellers waved bamboo fans in a half-hearted attempt to divert the flies. Chicken, beef, and pork I recognized, but what were the others. Horse? Dog? I didn't want to know, and I certainly never bought any. What I did buy I purchased early in the day, and quickly took home to refrigerate as I always worried about meat sold late in the afternoon after many hours of sitting in the heat.

My favorite area was the fruit display, where I discovered new delicious tastes. One enormous papaya, peeled, sliced, and refrigerated, provided me with a week of juicy, sweet breakfasts, and soft, ripe mangoes filled with sticky rice and coconut sauce soon became a favorite dessert. The season was never long enough to grant me my fill of juicy lamyai. Two other delightful treats were mangosteens, with their tangy apple flavor, and lychee, not pretty, but thoroughly delectable.

Large green, warty durian fruit was tasty, but the foul smell kept me from keeping it in my house. I had to laugh when I learned that you weren't allowed to take it into any hotel in Thailand.

Australian apples looked tempting, but they were so expensive that when I had to take a small gift to a party, I often took one or two of them as a treat.

To shop for vegetables, I carried a basket and plastic bags from home. I was expected to pick out my own tomatoes, corn, or beans from their attractive arrangement on bamboo trays, and lay them on the small round tin held out by the seller. She would then put my selection on her scale and quote me a price. This was one place where bargaining was unacceptable.

Vegetable market

This enchanting city of contrasts filled me with awe, wonder, and excitement, and the warm welcome from the international community made me quickly feel at home. I now knew that the decision I had made to come to Thailand was the right one. I felt strangely comfortable that this was the place for me to follow my pilgrimage.

DARA ACADEMY

My month of sightseeing was up. It was time to begin teaching. Looking back I still can't believe how quickly I had accepted the job to teach high school girls in a foreign country, in a school I knew nothing about! I was a fourth grade teacher in an upper-class suburban community in northern California. What did I know about Thailand, about a city called Chiang Mai, and a school called Dara Academy? What was an "academy" anyway? After saying "yes" I had begun my search for information and found very little. What I did learn was that if I wanted the position I would have to go on faith, and get answers along the way.

As I expected, mornings in the International School were just too much like teaching back in California. I was assigned a fourth grade classroom and started with only 13 students, a real plus after having classes of 30 to 40. But when I checked the makeup of my class I found I only had students from Australia, Iran, the United States, and Zimbabwe. Not even near the variety I had had back home.

When I saw my assigned textbooks, I was amazed to find they were the same I had previously used and another disappointment. Although this would make teaching much easier, I was here to have different experiences, something this definitely was not going to be.

Parents from the American Consulate arrived in our classrooms before school even began with offers to "help." I was uncomfortable with the many questions Donna and I were asked regarding our teaching and my antenna lighted up as I recognized some overly concerned parents. I didn't need this and felt uncomfortable with the possibility of too much parent involvement.

The staff was international with teachers from Australia, Tasmania, Thailand, and the United States, and I knew I would certainly enjoy working with them, but still felt the compulsion to spend all my time in a Thai school with all Thai students and a Thai faculty.

In contrast, afternoons at Dara did live up to my expectations. The campus at Dara was impressive. There were 280 Thai teachers and now one *farang* (pronounced fa-rahng) which was the term for foreigner. The "academy" included 4,600 girls from kindergarten through high school and every age level occupied its own special section of the campus, each separated by expansive lawns and large flowering jacaranda trees. My most inspiring recollection was seeing each level standing at attention in front of its classroom building to begin each day with announcements, and the singing of the "King's Song." Those 4,600 girls in their colorful red skirts and white blouses, scattered around that magnificent campus enthusiastically singing to their King, never ceased to thrill me.

I found many things difficult at first but learning to "*wai*" was one of the hardest. Thais do not usually shake hands. Rather, the customary greeting was the *wai*, with hands raised as if in prayer. Since the higher the hands, the more respectful the *wai*, you could theoretically identify respective ranks when observing two people greet each other. But rank is a complicated matter in Thailand, involving such things as age, occupation, and social position, so for an outsider, it is enough to make the gesture.

Next I had to learn who *wais* to whom! Students were expected to *wai* to a teacher, but a teacher did not *wai* to a student. It also seemed I should not *wai* to servants or clerks in the market. I was always a bit hesitant about when to *wai* and how high. This did not seem to be a problem for the Thai children. The school had not had a farang teacher for several years, and so I was a bit of an oddity. During the first few weeks on campus, I would often hear running feet approaching from all directions. The younger students, upon spying this new teacher, would run from great distances just to pass me, turn and *wai*, always with a smile and a giggle. Such fun!

Thai wai

I soon learned NOT to walk through the kindergarten play area during recess, for there I was mobbed by children. They were not concerned about *waiing*, but were eager to touch me. I found it difficult to stay on my feet with 80 or 100 little ones crowding around and pressing against me.

I was assigned to teach English to "Mauteum Hah", or M/5, which is equivalent to juniors in an American high school. Because school curriculum was directed from Bangkok, all students of each level had the same books so, although my classes had been studying the language for approximately nine years, they were much better at reading and writing than comprehension and speaking. After realizing this I felt my main job was to allow them to hear English from a native English speaker. My first surprise came when many students seemed confused with my directions and I soon learned that Thai English teachers usually gave directions in Thai, and required English only when using the text. Students were not used to being told in English to, "Pick up your book, turn to page 82, and we'll start with paragraph six."

Because I had a difficult time learning the Thai language, the students were challenged by hearing only English from me. In Thai, a monosyllabic language, there are five different tones—high, medium, low, rising or falling to distinguish between words. For example, the word "mai" could have five completely different meanings depending on the tone used. Therefore, when I did try to speak Thai I was very careful. I knew I had made a mistake when I told one class, in Thai, that my elder sister was coming to visit me. Their laughter was a clue that I had not said "sister." I had used a rising tone instead of the correct falling tone, and ended up telling them that my "ghost" was coming!

There was always a lot of giggling in my classroom, as I tried to have a good time with my girls, hoping they would relax and not be too awed by this *farang* teacher. After a while, however, I began to realize that this giggling was often a sign of nervousness or embarrassment. At first no one raised a hand or asked a question, and I learned that teachers were held in such high esteem that students were too embarrassed to ask anything which would imply ignorance. The ESL books told me to get the students talking! Easier said than done.

Thai names are very long and easy to mispronounce, an awkward mistake in any language, so I decided that I would offer the girls English names for our classes. They were delighted with this idea, so I quickly compiled a huge list of my favorites, which I wrote on the blackboard. Each student was then allowed to choose the one she wanted. I soon found that Sara, Ruth, Ann, Esther, and Jane were not a bit popular. Preferred names must end with the sound of an *e*. Thus, the ones chosen first were Cindy, Julie, Christy, Mindy, or any name of a current popular young Hollywood movie star.

I decided that assigned seats and charts were a must. I had five classes, each with fifty girls; fifty girls the same age, approximately the same size, all with short dark hair, most with bangs, and all in white blouses and red skirts. Multiply these fifty by five classes, and realize that I had 250 girls who looked very much alike to me. Those seating charts were my salvation.

I soon learned to enjoy and appreciate the traditions of the Thai classroom where I was now called *acharn*, not teacher. When I appeared in front of the class, the "lead student" would lean forward and *wai* with the others, as they all said, "Good morning, Acharn Jackie. How are you?" I would respond, "I am fine, thank you, and you?" and they replied, "We are fine, thank you." Now I could begin.

The rooms I taught in were rather bare. There were a few windows with shutters, but no glass and the lights were seldom turned on, even on dark, rainy days. Because we were in a semi-tropical zone, there was no heating system, and layered clothing was the answer during the cold, wet months. My high school girls remained in the classroom with the shutters closed during this time but I would often see the elementary school teachers holding their classes outside on the lawns using the sun for warmth. The little ones were a delightful sight, bundled up in knit hats, mufflers, and colorful sweaters, sitting in the sun on small chairs lined up in rows.

One tradition I really appreciated was that the last class of the day cleaned the classroom. As soon as a teacher finished the lesson, everyone was up doing something. Shutters were closed, brooms quickly swept the floors, trash was taken out, desks straightened, blackboards cleaned, erasers clapped, and in a very few minutes the room was ready for a new day.

I was disturbed when I first noticed one of the girls with her head down on her desk, obviously not paying attention and possibly asleep. Naturally this would not be acceptable in a classroom in the States and when I asked what the problem was, I was quietly informed that the student was sick. Since this was a private school and it was a real sacrifice for some parents to get their daughters into Dara, it was unthinkable that they would not attend every day. Thus, all the girls came, well or not, and teachers allowed them to sleep or rest as needed.

All tests were given at the same time and I soon learned how important they were. For final exams, the girls sat in the large chapel, desks spaced apart, monitors constantly patrolling the aisles. Making up my tests and exams was a trying ordeal. I wanted to be fair, and so I tried to replicate what the Thai English teachers were doing. My first tests seemed far too hard, but I was assured they were fine. The system allowed for students to keep taking an exam until they passed. No one failed. The teacher simply made the exam easier each time.

Extra classes were also held on Saturday mornings and Wednesday afternoons to help failing students. There were no set working hours for teachers. They just appeared and did what had to be done, even if it meant teaching on holidays, Saturdays, or after school. I never heard a complaint. Correcting 250 exams at a time was a new experience for me. We were encouraged to have multiple choice, some fill-in and a few essay questions. No teacher's aides to help correct and grade papers here!

However, I enjoyed doing it, especially trying to figure out exactly what the students meant. When one answered, "You would expect floor to floor carpeting in the office," I presumed she meant, "wall-to-wall carpeting." Another said, "I'm going to step on my foot!" when she meant, "I'm going to put my foot down." I wasn't sure about, "Every day the telephone leaves the hospital for trips to the restaurant," or "Henry could not cross the road quickly now because he died."

Soon teachers from other grade levels began inviting me to visit their classrooms to teach their students songs and games. The younger children especially enjoyed learning and playing "The Farmer in the Field" (they did not understand "dell"), and the Hokey Pokey.

A number of the young male teachers had formed a popular combo that played at various school celebrations. But, while they had access to popular American songs, they could not always decipher the words. Therefore, I found myself sitting in front of my tape deck, many an evening, trying to understand those words myself so I could help them. Our pop singers do not always pronounce words carefully, and I had to listen to some tapes ten or twenty times.

Near the end of my first semester, the school manager suggested that I start working with nine elementary school English teachers, giving them pointers on teaching English. We made plans for them to come to a class after school on Monday, but only four showed up. I decided that what I really needed was to see what was going on in their classrooms, so I would know how to help them. Reluctantly, they gave me a schedule, and I began visiting five or six a week. This was an uncomfortable situation for I know I was threatening to them—me a *farang*, watching them teach my language.

I found that most of the teachers did a commendable job although their pronunciation left much to be desired. One primary teacher was teaching the word *old*. She would say OL and then spell it with the class, "O L D"—emphasizing the D in the spelling but never pronouncing it. Another teacher kept pronouncing policeMAN as policeMEN. When I mentioned it to her, she showed me her manual which said: "policeMAN was pronounced policeMEN." This was typical of Thai English books. I had an answer book to one of my readers, and could generally count on three or four out of eight comprehension questions being answered incorrectly. Often two answers were so close it was hard to decide, and the students were told to pick the BEST. I spent much time preparing my conferences with these teachers but, as with the students, it was difficult to get them to ask questions. They too, did not want to suggest that they did not know something.

What impressed me most about Dara and Thai students was their great motivation to learn. Parents really instilled in them the belief that the only way to succeed in this developing country was to become educated. School started at 8 a.m. and closed at 3:35 p.m. for all classes from first grade on, with most of the day spent on academics. Because of the large size of the classes, much of the teaching in primary grades was done by rote. As I walked around campus I would hear whole classes reading a story together, or reciting a lesson in unison. Only recently had there been concern about helping the individual child. Thai teachers were very dedicated. A great number of girls who dreamed of attending one of Thailand's few universities hurried to buses at the end of the day, heading for private tutoring classes downtown.

Being a teacher in Thailand was a unique experience. When introduced as an "Acharn," one immediately gained respect and was regarded, someone told me, as slightly below royalty. There were never any discipline problems; it would be unthinkable for a Thai student to show disrespect to a teacher. I liked that. Would I be able to come down off this pedestal when I returned home?

MAI PEN RAI

One of the first phrases I learned during Thai language studies was *mai pen rai* which means "never mind" or, "not to worry, everything's o.k.". Thai Buddhists know that anxiety and fretting are unhealthy so they truly practice 'flowing with life,' and remaining calm when plans suddenly change or life takes a new turn. Although *mai pen rai* became my favorite Thai phrase, I found its advice difficult to follow, but persevered because I knew it to be a wonderful lesson for a highly structured farang to learn. Dara Academy was the perfect place to practice.

When my sister and son visited me for a month, they had planned their trip to fall between terms while students were on vacation. Before they arrived I had conscientiously spent hours getting lesson plans and dittos ready for the first week of the new term. That first Monday morning after the holiday I headed for school eager and ready to teach. Surprise! No need to teach this week. All the girls would be busy getting ready for the big fair on Saturday. Since this was the major fund raising event of the year, of course it superseded classes.

Then I discovered that the fair really started on Wednesday. It took place out on the school grounds but unfortunately rain began to pour Wednesday morning and didn't let up for the rest of the week. The grounds became a quagmire, a situation in which everything would certainly have been canceled in California, but here the soaked students continued to throw darts at balloons, cook food, etc. No reason to stop because of a little rain. *Mai pen rai!*

Then it was "Parent's Day" at the fair and I was sure things would slow down, but no, it just meant that more people were throwing darts, eating, and walking in the mud. In addition to various booths for games, skills, and food, there was what I thought the best part, the stage show put on by the girls. How I did enjoy their dancing, singing, and drama presentations! The stage had been built in the middle of the large central lawn and these beautiful, talented young ladies looked quite professional in their colorful, traditional Thai dresses. They must have been practicing since birth the way they were able to bend their fingers back, Thai style, at a most unnatural but very necessary angle to achieve the required effect.

Another "surprise" arrived before the week was over. On Friday I was handed an entirely new schedule for the new term. There went my nice lesson plans and carefully prepared dittos. One English teacher had suddenly quit so I was asked to cover half her classes. I was delighted to do this, for I felt I had not contributed enough to the school and was feeling a little sad that time was flying and I was just beginning to catch on to the system. Was I learning *mai pen rai*? Indeed I was! Now I was afraid I was becoming so flexible I would have difficulty adjusting back to the very organized American school system.

Every few weeks there seemed to be another special day or special week, and Sport's Day turned out to be one of my favorites. As I entered my office after lunch one afternoon, I was handed a t-shirt stenciled with a delightful picture of children playing at Dara. Every student and teacher in the school was assigned to a different team: yellow, red, blue, green, or mine, the purple. It was an amazing sight when Sport's Day finally arrived to see 4,600 students from kindergarten through high school, wearing their team's colorful shirt.

The day began with Acharn Rojana picking me up early Friday morning on her motorcycle. We drove to the train station maneuvering through heavy morning traffic with my arms firmly encircling Acharn's waist and my eyes tightly closed. The statistics on motorcycle accidents in Chiang Mai gave me good reason to be unnerved. When we safely pulled up to the crowded station, I was delighted to see the third grade girls lined up and ready to march down the street playing their song flutes. They were dressed in attractive military-type red and white uniforms and proud tall hats with white plumes. Behind them was the Dara marching band, also dressed in attractive red and white, ready to parade. Soon cars and buses, samlors and seelars had all stopped and, with Dara parents following and cheering along the way, the parade set off, song flutes tooting and band playing. We joined the confusion and proceeded for several blocks down one of the busiest streets in town.

Sports Day Parade

When we turned into the crowded main yard at Dara, more girls were lined up behind their colors. Balloons and streamers marked the various teams and after everyone had sung the King's Song, colorful smoke bombs filled the air with violet, yellow, red, blue, and green smoke. Sports Day had begun.

Two hundred five and six year olds, doing calisthenics together in the Kindergarten yard was impressive and I was amazed to see these young children exercising with such precision. A lot of work must have gone into learning these skills.

Each grade level had different competitions in different areas spread throughout the campus. I spent a lot of time watching the third grade girls play "basket" basketball and couldn't wait to get back home to teach this fun game to my American students. It consisted of two teams trying to make points. However, the basket was not stationary. One student stood on a chair holding up a wicker basket and moving it to catch the ball if the thrower did not aim accurately.

The high school girls had recruited some of their younger sisters as cheerleaders. These little girls carried colorful pompoms and wore special cheerleader outfits to match the team they were supporting and it was obvious from the originality of their cheers and routines that they, too, had been practicing.

The volleyball competition was fiercely competitive. I had watched the girls practice during PE periods and realized that physical education was taken very seriously in Thailand. Now as I watched their keen playing skills I could imagine I was at a National Championship.

Another surprise awaited me several weeks later when I entered my office. I was told to get a sleeping bag and pack warm clothes ready for Girl Scout Camp. Every grade level in the school belonged to some organization and on different days I saw students wearing Red Cross, Girl Guide, or Girl Scout uniforms. I really looked forward to this upcoming experience.

On Saturday I was driven to the camp only thirty minutes from Dara, in the foothills of Doi Sutep, the mountain behind Chiang Mai. This was the most beautiful scout camp I had ever seen. It was in a heavily wooded area, with a waterfall and creek running through the middle of the grounds. Cabins were on different levels, but within easy climbing distance of each other, and as we looked down from the mountain we enjoyed a spectacular view of Chiang Mai and the plains beyond.

Since we were up several thousand feet, the temperature dropped quickly as the sun began to set and suddenly the area became a colorful mosaic as the girls donned bright warm knitted caps and scarves.

I soon found myself with the other teachers sitting on a cabin porch enjoying a tasty Thai dinner, evidence that our school cook had also been invited to Girl Scout camp. All around us on the mountainside fires blazed as the girls from each cabin prepared their own meal.

I looked forward to the campfire hour with happy memories

of my own scouting experiences. Everyone gathered around an enormous bonfire and enjoyed the heat of the flames as night temperatures continued to drop. I snuggled into my jacket, glad of my cozy hat, scarf, and gloves and realized it was the first time I had actually felt cold since arriving in Thailand.

The girls were well prepared for the campfire program with skits, songs, and games. The dark hillside rang with their laughter and applause and then came the highlight of the evening. The Scout Leader suggested they needed to warm up and suddenly the air exploded with American musical tapes and the girls jumped to their feet. Social dancing anywhere else is strictly forbidden to a Dara girl, so they flung themselves enthusiastically into this once a year treat. I couldn't help thinking some were so good, they obviously didn't dance just once a year. American dances mixed with Thai dances and I was coaxed to my feet and felt quite foolish as the girls, with lots of laughter and giggles, tried to teach me how to bend my fingers back and coordinate body, feet, and hands in a Thai posture. While I was embarrassed, the girls seemed pleased that I made the effort.

As the evening progressed I became tired and ready to hear the call for taps. The chilly night air and lateness of the hour made me long for my sleeping bag, but now I found one profound difference between American and Thai scout camps. In the States scouts were sent to bed at a reasonable hour. In Thailand, the object was to keep the campfire going as long as possible to get the girls so tired they would pile into bed crying for sleep.

The unwelcome call for calisthenics awoke me at 5:30 a.m. It was dark and cold so I ignored it and went back to sleep. When I appeared at 7:30 a.m., breakfast was well under way and a group of girls were already cleaning the camp area. Later in the morning I walked around camp observing as each patrol marched to ten different "posts," at each of which a scout leader gave a five to seven minute talk on some aspect of camping, health, or safety.

Sharing this camp with girls from a very different culture, halfway around the world from my home, but with the same interests and goals, was a thoroughly enjoyable experience for me. We can't be so very far apart when we all learn the same Scout laws.

Later in the month, and before leaving school on a Thursday afternoon, another surprise! I was told to forget my lesson plans for the following day and to wear "work clothes." Upon arriving at school the next morning, the red and white school uniforms had disappeared and I was startled to see all the young girls in jeans and denim shirts. I hesitantly appeared in my own jeans feeling strange not to be wearing the traditional Dara Friday uniform for teachers: a red skirt, white blouse, and white jacket with a Dara emblem on the pocket. This was Work Day.

Acharn Naraporn said I was to be her assistant and our job was to remove a large pile of cleared brush from the front of the school campus to a trash area in the rear. Girls appeared with gloves and wheelbarrows and the work began. The gardeners had obviously prepared for this day because we found a huge pile of shrubs and tree cuttings and we all had a good time clearing the area. We pushed our wheelbarrows full of trimmings past students who were landscaping a small garden area. Six of them tried to push an enormous rock into the right place while others planted flowers, shrubs and bulbs. Next we passed classrooms where all the desks and tables had been moved out. I was amazed and impressed to see the teacher and students on hands and knees with a bucket of soapy water scrubbing the floor.

Enjoying Work Day

In the afternoon when all the chores were finished, a festive atmosphere was in the air. Students walked around inspecting the results of their work, sitting in groups, singing, and just enjoying themselves. At the end of that Friday we left a sparkling clean campus. Many hours of paid labor had been saved, the students had had fun and had learned how productive they could be. I liked Work Day.

With each passing week, I became more adept at accepting and practicing the *mai pen rai* philosophy. Now I could take it easy, slow down, not sweat the small stuff. In fact I was even beginning to feel quite comfortable with the unexpected. I think this all comes naturally to the Thai culture encouraged by the hot weather and teachings of Buddha. The phrase *mai pen rai* was now a natural part of my vocabulary and way of life, too.

And yet, why does this not carry over to the small study group I attend each week? It is always a disturbing experience! The evening is shared with great, caring people who know why I have come to Thailand. But, it is so embarrassing to find myself weeping at each session. We are reading a book by a Yale professor about his search for meaning in life. It seems that while I have been in Thailand, everything I have read gives me new insight into things I should have done to help Lee.

I had never heard of "co-dependency" before, that situation where one person lets the other lean on him, thus not allowing that person to stand on his own two feet and make decisions for himself. I now realize that I was the master "co-dependent." I was always trying to do things for Lee, trying to ease his physical and emotional pain. Obviously it didn't work. I always felt I was walking a tight rope—trying to do the right thing and yet never really getting it.

I recall the time when we took Lee to live with his aunt where the climate was better for his arthritis and where his doctor cousin could take over his treatment. I still had to teach so could only take the train every Friday evening to spend Saturday and Sunday with him. Lee was in the middle of his recovery, still having difficulty moving and walking. I felt so guilty being away from him all week that as soon as I arrived, I began to help him dress, put on his shoes that were so hard to reach, doing everything that was an effort for him.

I'll never forget the weekend that his cousin took me aside and suggested that I not be such a big help when I came. He said that Lee's condition always regressed after my visits because he did not do things for himself. He needed that struggle to help in his recovery. How could I have been so dumb?

It is hard now to look back and see the mistakes I made in my effort "to do what was right." With each new insight there is the pain that I should have known. Where was all this knowledge and information when I needed it? There are now so many new books on depression and recovery. Why weren't they available for me?

Where is mai pen rai when I really need it?

THE LONG ROAD
TO BAW GAO

My teaching responsibilities at the two schools kept me busy Monday through Friday. However, on my weekends I was free to do as I chose. Thus I found myself one hot, humid Friday afternoon, again riding in the back of a covered pick-up truck bouncing over more rugged Thai mountain roads. Squeezed in with me on the two hard narrow benches that lined the sides of the vehicle were nine beautiful young Thai student nurses.

I had eagerly accepted the invitation from Dr. Sukett, the world renowned nose and throat doctor, to be part of a Thai-International volunteer medical team of twenty-six from McCormick Hospital in Chiang Mai. It was an honor to be asked by this new friend and I recalled how gracious he was when we first met and how he had then encouraged me to "come along and see the program." He had told me how each month he took a medical team to one of the thirteen outlying provinces where there were neither hospitals nor doctors. Here they tended to the tribal people who continually suffered from chronic ear problems and other illnesses related to the damp cold winter spent in their open houses high in the mountains.

It had all sounded so innocent when I was told that it was "just" a three hour drive from Chiang Mai to Baw Gao through dense rain forests and over breath-taking mountains. When I took out my map Baw Gao was nowhere to be found.

Dr. Sukett was anxious for his student nurses to spend some time with this farang and asked me to sit in the back of the truck with them, so I came prepared. My worn Thai language book was handy in my shirt pocket, my head filled with ideas for songs, and my small tape recorder set so we could sing and record. Thai girls, too, like to hear themselves on tape.

We started by exchanging names as we rattled northwest from Chiang Mai; names like Nickie, Nu, Chung, Air, Joy, Im, Cy, Ay, and Aw. Even though these were considerably easier to remember than their real six to seven syllable Thai names, I still had trouble keeping Ay and Aw apart.

Very soon I discovered that each girl had brought along at least one bag of goodies. I continued to be amazed at how the Thai females' figures remained so slim and willowy, even though they seemed to eat all day long. Within five minutes of leaving the hospital, the girls were passing around their bags of "kanoms" (Thai sweets)—gluay (crispy bananas that had been sliced and deep fried), tua dut (crunchy peanut brittle, just like at home), various flavored fruity cookies, and a sticky figgy candy. Much too sweet for me this early in the morning, but I ate!

The girls were friendly and eager to sing for my tape recorder. First came an old Thai folk song. Thoughtfully a tall and serene young lady named Joy, who spoke the best English and seemed to be spokesperson for the group, explained the song to me. It was about people who lived in a beautiful forest and enjoyed peace and happiness. As my Thai was still as limited as their English, this made the trip and our time together even more interesting.

We discovered that we all knew "Old MacDonald Had a Farm," but soon broke up laughing as we argued about the sounds the animals made. They would not agree with me that a cow says "moo!" And certainly pigs would never say "oink!" They insisted that their cows made a sound more like "ur-uh," and their pigs communicated with a "gr-ent."

Soon we turned off the busy paved road out of Chiang Mai onto a winding mountain track that was under construction. As dust began to pour in through the open windows, the girls passed out white gauze surgical caps and we quickly tucked our hair out of sight. Next we covered our noses and mouths with heavy cotton surgical masks as the thick red dust made it difficult to breathe. Obviously these student nurses knew about Thai mountain roads and had come prepared. It must have been a bizarre sight to see these ten women crunched together in the back of a small covered truck, heads and mouths protected by gauze made red with dust. To add to this peculiar scene, the girls began to get motion sickness so they laid their heads on each other's shoulders and sat stacked like a deck of cards. A particularly brutal bump shook them alert and they soundlessly reshuffled their positions.

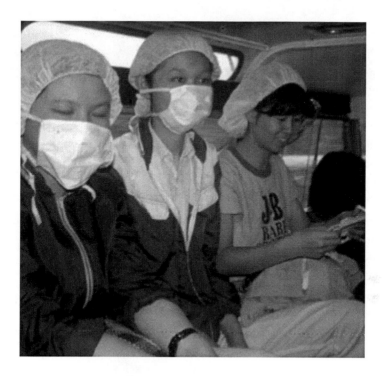

Dusty ride to Baw Gao

I had been delegated to the back with them so I could visit and get acquainted. So much for any of that now. As the road became more difficult, it was hard work just to stay in our tiny allotted space. Using the power of positive thinking, I calmed my queezy stomach and concentrated on the rest of me: legs that cramped because they could not move, knuckles white and sore from gripping the narrow rail or back door, arms that felt as if they were being torn out of their sockets, and my poor back aching from being braced so I would not tumble off the narrow seat. I frantically estimated the hours left, unable to tell time because watch and glasses were covered with that dreadful dust.

Hot and thirsty I began to dream of those wonderful roadside stops back in California where, in a building shaped like a Giant Orange, enormous glasses of crushed ice were filled with delicious, sweet, fresh orange juice. My dream was cut short when our truck suddenly skidded to a halt. We looked out at a dusty village of four bamboo houses and a market consisting of an open shelter with a few items laid out on a plank. Of oranges there was no sign, in fact there was nothing at all in the way of a thirst-quenching drink. Therefore I turned my attention to another beautiful view of Northern Thailand: the narrow, rocky dirt road, crooked stick fences, green patches of rice fields, the ever-present muddy water buffalo snoozing in the shade and the dark green teak forests outlining the horizon. The startlingly clear skies here dazzled me in contrast to the smoky haze which curtained the mountains around Chiang Mai. It was the constant burning along city roads and fields that destroyed that city's magnificent view, and I could never accept the people's casual attitude regarding pollution in this beautiful country.

We crowded back into our truck with the disheartening information we were only halfway to our destination. I found that closing my eyes and pretending to be relaxed helped ease the misery. As the miles crawled by, the confined space, the hot, sticky weather, and the bouncing motion lulled us all close to a state of unconsciousness.

Suddenly we were startled by a voice announcing "Baw Gao"! The truck slowed to a halt and I stood up eager to get out and explore. But what did I see? On a slight rise above a verdant valley sat a large, square, dark brown teak house. When I turned to see the rest of Baw Gao I discovered only a small meandering creek and a blue lake made by a defunct tin-mining operation. So this was it: a wide spot on a dusty mountain road, with a house on a hill. I hadn't known what to expect, but it wasn't this!

Within a short time twenty-six of us were sitting on the cool floor of the teak house eating our evening meal of steamed rice, small pieces of boiled meat, and crunchy snow peas on banana leaves. After the banana leaves were cleared away we sang more American folk songs. Everyone was familiar with them as they were always taught in the Thai English classes—but they didn't know the Hokey Pokey! It was quite a sight to see the doctors and dentists joining in the fun, and all were soon giggling as they put their "back sides in!" Everyone seemed to know the words to "London Bridge is Falling Down" but didn't realize it was a game. "Why does it fall down?" "How do we make a bridge?" Soon this international group of professionals were unselfconsiously skipping around the room and "under the bridge" to "take the key and lock them up."

The evening ended with a stroll around the quiet lake which glimmered under a full moon. I spent most of the walk answering questions from the student nurses about my country. "What is San Francisco really like? Are the hills slippery? Do you have a big house? Do you know any movie stars? Tell us about your son and daughter." A feeling of melancholy came over me as we walked under the stars in this strange, faraway place. I felt I was in another world and at that moment home seemed very far away.

Because I was the senior member of the group, I was given the one bed in the house. However, that meant that I had to share it with the two women doctors who were part of our team. The problem of three in a bed was quickly solved by our sleeping crosswise. So, in a narrow bed in the quiet mountains of Northern Thailand there could soon be heard the gentle breathing of one doctor from Thailand, one doctor from Australia, and one tired schoolteacher from California.

BAW GAO COMES ALIVE

It was five o'clock the next morning when I was gently awakened from a sound sleep by the student nurses inviting me to join them for an early walk. I crept out of bed without disturbing my sleeping partners and slipped into warm clothes, for my nose already tingled from the crisp mountain air. I joined the others who waited for me by the lake. A low mist hung over the water and together we watched the pale yellow moon disappear, chased by a rosy glow in the east which grew brighter and pinker until the glorious red ball of the tropical sun slid into view.

We began to walk, following the white smoke of our breath, and I was again grateful for that soft knitted hat, colorful scarf and cozy mittens I had bought in the Chiang Mai market. I could see traces of starched white nurse's blouses and slacks peeking from under my companions' heavy jackets and knew they would soon be busy at work.

Back at the house, casting aside a lifelong habit of cornflake breakfasts, I devoured with gusto the savory, hot rice gruel that included bits of green spinach and chunks of crisp, fried, dry fish. It was nourishing, tasty, and filling, and after a cup of hot tea I was ready for anything.

Outside I found our international medical team already setting up on the only clear, level space in this heavily wooded area—an old basketball court next to the house. Their equipment consisted of a few long folding tables to hold supplies, and some rather decrepit chairs for people to sit on during examinations.

Medical team

The dentist was busy sweeping out the small wooden shack at the edge of the clearing and arranging his equipment; a rusty, dented bucket and another old chair. Because of the lack of electricity he had been unable to bring any of his dental equipment so he would give each patient a shot of novocain, pull out any diseased or bad teeth and drop them into the bucket. Privately I swore never to complain of going to my own dentist again!

Before all preparations were finished the ever-present Thai vendors appeared, each quickly claiming a small patch of ground at the edge of the clearing. There some spread simple straw mats or pieces of tattered canvas, others had brought crude tables or wooden planks and black iron pots for cooking. In no time any food one could find at a large Thai market was available and the mountain air filled with succulent aromas. There was kow tom (thick rice soup with chicken), mii grawp (crispy yellow noodles), small, sweet, crunchy waffles, and Kow neo, my favorite, sticky rice. In addition to drinks and packaged junk foods there were all the delicious Thai fruits: lumyai, ramutams, durian, and plenty of juicy watermelon slices which I enjoyed before the flies took over. I continued to be careful about what I ate in any market place and hoped I did not offend anyone.

In the midst of this busy scene I was saddened to see so many children selling these wares, realizing they would never attend school but spend their lives living in these mountains eking out a difficult hand-to-mouth existence.

For two weeks before our arrival a pickup truck with loudspeaker equipment had driven over the many narrow mountain roads announcing the annual medical visit. These isolated people had met Dr. Sukett and his team regularly over the past ten years and knew that shots for their children and medicine for the sick were essential, so I knew these tribal families would soon be arriving.

I couldn't wait to see these people whose ancestors had migrated from Southern China into Thailand hundreds of years before. Thailand has many varied cultures, but next to the predominant Thais there are six groups called the Hilltribe people who live simply and poorly in villages in this Northern region. I had seen a few representatives of these Hmong, Karen, Mien, Lahu, Akha, and Lisu in the refugee camps and markets of Chiang Mai and had been fascinated by them and their clothing. Each tribe made theirs unique by the addition of coins, shells, colored beads, and silvery jewelry or bright colored yarn. Now I would see them in their natural habitat.

And they came, seeming to swarm out of nowhere like hundreds of ants to a sticky sweet. As I walked down the road to watch their arrival I was amazed that the area which had a few moments before looked unpopulated was now alive with people emerging from the trees and down the dusty road. They sauntered as though headed to a fair, smiling happily and greeting friends. Their bright outfits glistened in the brilliant morning sun. Occasionally a path was cleared for three or four people on one motorcycle to wind precariously through the crowd. I gasped when I saw thirty or forty people holding onto each other, standing closely packed in the bed of a pickup truck as it crept carefully over the crest of the hill. After it had discharged its passengers the driver was off for another load.

Everyone had put on their best, but I especially liked the dresses worn by a group of Hmong women. The basic cloth was a black woven material with accents of brilliant pink. Many silver-like decorations were attached at random and long pink yarn pompoms dangled from the backs of their belts. Around their necks the women wore layered silver coils and silver bracelets encircled their arms. Their shiny black hair, which had never been cut, was piled high into a bun on top of their heads.

One of the staff later told me that these clothes were only purchased when they celebrated the New Year after which the proud owners would wear the same outfit continuously for several years, day and night. Their fresh, sparkly look would begin to fade in a month or two. I had seen some of these discarded, old, worn garments being sold in the Night Market for many baht to eager tourists.

Quietly each new arrival found a place in line. Mothers anxiously comforted their babies and small children as the student nurses prepared the shots. I helped where I could, impressed by the caring, efficiency, and skill of these young women as they gave all manner of injections.

Shots. Shots. Shots. Pills. Pills. Pills. As I watched those lovely nurses giving shots, I remembered the thousands of needles stuck in Lee over the years. It was especially bad in the year leading up to that Christmas vacation when he went to bed. It seemed that we were constantly heading to the hospital for something called "gold shots" for his arthritis, then massive doses of cortisone, and as his knees filled up with liquid, huge needles were inserted to remove fluid. That was something I could not watch.

When I took over his care that Christmas I had to phone the doctor every day to report on his condition, then administer the shots prescribed: penicillin shots in his hip, B-12 shots in his arm and then the difficult daily antigen shots carefully slid under the skin. If a bubble did not appear, I had to try again. In addition there were the regular blood transfusions because of his anemia—and more needles.

Even when he was able to walk again and return to work, the pills at the breakfast table filled a small bowl. When I think back on the fact that Lee started taking medications in his teen years, it is amazing to me that a body could absorb all those chemicals and not be affected. Could this be a cause for depression?

While the pills and shots got Lee back on his feet, the pain never completely subsided. From his teens to his death, Lee was never free from some kind of pain. He was very stoic about it and seldom mentioned it. But did it finally get to him? Was it finally too much to bear?

"Come Acharn Jackie. We need your help!" It took four of us to hold down one thrashing baby. After that vaccination was finally completed the mother refused to subject her infant to a second and was ready to take him away. Gently and with understanding the nurse convinced her how important it was and eventually she relented. It was quickly over and the mother left grateful and smiling.

I saw frustration in the anxious faces of two young medical interns from the University of Chicago who were in training at McCormick Hospital. It must have been difficult to adapt their Western training to these very different symptoms and I guessed how each day in Thailand must foster a stronger awareness of the public's need for more knowledge in regard to sanitation and diet.

Even seasoned Thai doctors found it hard to prescribe medications as they made educated guesses without the back-up of a medical lab. I was disheartened when I heard one doctor tell a young mother that her badly deformed baby needed immediate attention and must be taken to the hospital in Chiang Mai. She sadly shook her head, indicated that she already had too many children, and quietly walked away.

Adding to the difficulty of treating these people in this isolated mountain area was the problem of communication. Each tribe had its own language and only a few understood Thai. Although interpreters tried to help, sign language and facial expressions often proved the best way to get the meaning across.

The medical team worked throughout the day with only short breaks and finally stopped at dusk for supper. As we gathered to eat, the dentist arrived announcing his bucket count as having reached one hundred and sixty teeth. Suddenly my appetite faltered.

Darkness fell and I heard the roar of a generator. Movie time! The tribal people huddled expectantly under thick blankets, sitting on the old basketball court. Meanwhile, around the edge, the shot team and clinic reopened for business which was still brisk. I was called on to hold a flashlight so the nurses could see. When I glanced over at the film I was surprised by the sight and sound of Billy Graham talking in Thai. Of course the audience couldn't understand a word he said, but for them even watching this inappropriate movie was a unique opportunity.

At ten after ten, film, lanterns, and flashlights were extinguished. Vendors had packed up their wares and, while we headed wearily for our house, hundreds of people melted silently into the darkness of the night.

FORBIDDEN FIELDS

The room was dark and cold when I awoke our third day in Baw Gao. I snuggled under the blankets absorbing the warmth that radiated from the two doctors who slept quietly beside me. The house was still yet I thrilled to a sense of anticipation. Something special was happening today. What was it? My mind gradually focused and I remembered. We were going to visit the opium fields of the famous Golden Triangle.

How many times had I read about these plants in the *San Francisco Chronicle* or heard about the problems they caused as reported on the evening news. Just before heading to Thailand, there had been a feature article in the Sunday paper, written by a young journalist who had visited this infamous area, a startling accomplishment as these places were carefully guarded and difficult to find.

Thailand's opium fields are one of the world's main suppliers of the drug, a source of both money and death. Millions of dollars are made on this crop and millions of lives lost. I was both excited and apprehensive about our visit.

Because Dr. Sukett had been there many times and was a trusted friend of the tribal people, one of them had offered to take us, but first we had a morning of patients to see.

I was also looking forward to attending the Sunday worship service at the local Karen Christian Church to which we had all been invited. As a child in a little Baptist Church in Illinois I had heard about these Karens. They were one of the church's most important mission projects and our Sunday School classes would often read reports about this "far off place" and put our pennies and change in little cardboard banks to help those foreign people. How strange that I would now be visiting one of those very churches. The Karens had one of the largest Christian populations of any tribal people with their churches scattered throughout the mountains.

While we finished up our morning's work, Dr. Sukett was off in the hills cutting down bamboo to be used as edging for his exquisite garden in Chiang Mai. Just as we were about to leave for the church service he appeared, elated, with a handful of tiny, wiggly bamboo worms which he had found in one of the sections of bamboo. Evidently the Thais consider these a rare and tasty treat but he put them away until later and joined the twenty-six of us as we trudged up the hill to attend this Christian worship service. Several of the Thai in our group were Buddhists. One doctor had spoken of her Catholic faith and probably the majority were atheists. We may even have had a Muslim but it didn't matter. How typically Thai to do the polite thing. We were invited so everyone went.

As we entered the simple bamboo, thatched-roof church in the clearing on the far side of the hill, we split up, the men to one side, the women and children to the other. Our shoes had been left behind at the bottom of the ladder we had climbed to enter the large, square room which was six feet above the ground.

We joined the group already sitting on the floor and I tried to find a comfortable position for my legs. Would I ever be able to sit this way and not be in agony in a very short time? Thai culture finds feet offensive. They are never to be pointed in the direction of another person and though when I first arrived in Thailand this custom was impressed upon me I still found it difficult to uphold. How easy it was to push a lower drawer shut with one's foot. Not acceptable! The Thais would never forget the time President Lyndon Johnson visited Thailand and while talking with the King on television, crossed his legs and pointed his toe toward the ruler. The whole country gasped in unison. For myself I would always vividly and with agony, remember the day I teased another teacher in the office at our school and pretended to send a kick in her direction. This woman who was my closest friend, and always spoke with gentle kindness, reacted with shocked anger. "Why did you do that?" She had never spoken to me in that tone before and I was horrified when I realized what I had done. It was a simple, comical gesture in the United States, but totally unwelcome in Thailand. I never pointed my toe at anyone again. And now I sat with my legs aching, but correctly folded beneath me.

The congregation was delighted to have us join them and their smiling faces radiated greetings, so we felt very welcome. The Karen's favorite color is red, and though their beautifully woven clothing contained rich blues and yellows, red was always predominant and how cheerful it looked in this simple wooden building. Around their necks the women wore as many as 40 or 50 strands of tiny red and yellow beads and on their heads the turbans were of varied colors, mostly made of torn pieces of Turkish towels.

About one hundred people crowded together in this small building where the only decorations were a few Western-style religious pictures of Jesus, and Bible stories tacked to the bamboo walls. The leader who was responsible for a number of mountain churches stood at a simple wooden podium and began the service. He was probably a layman as there were not enough trained Karen ministers to regularly lead all the Sunday services.

While we could not understand the words spoken, some of us could join in during the hymns, as unfortunately, these people with such a rare and beautiful culture of their own had simply taken our traditional American hymns and translated them into their own language. Later, when I returned to Chiang Mai, a friend who taught music at a local University, assured me that an effort was being made to encourage them to take their splendid traditional music and develop their own hymns.

Why was everyone staring at me when we arrived back at the house for lunch? Then I saw Dr. Sukett heading toward me with a twinkle in his eye and a small bowl in his hand. The worms had returned, only this time they were sauteed. Since I was the senior honored guest with the group, he was giving me the privilege of eating this precious delicacy which he had prepared with great care. Twenty-five pair of eyes watched expectantly. What to do? Trying not to show my apprehension, I graciously thanked him, took a deep breath and popped the little creatures into my mouth. To my amazement I found them tasty, crunchy and very edible. Flavored with peanut oil, garlic, and spices they were like very small fried shrimp and the savory taste lingers in my mouth today. Now I am quick to agree with the Thai that bamboo worms are a delicacy.

As soon as lunch was over we headed up the steep mountainside road in several trucks while Dr. Sukett gave me background information regarding the growing of opium in Southeast Asia. The poppy is only produced by poor people, so the basic unit of cultivation and production is the farmer's family. The size of the plot is restricted to the number of plants that can be incised and then scraped within a twenty-four hour period. We were visiting this area during the critical harvest season.

The government of Thailand and the USDEA (United States Drug Enforcement Agency) had been very active in recent years, trying to curtail the growth of opium in Thailand so the biggest amount was being now grown in Burma. Thailand, however, was still the major transshipment route for the opium grown and for the morphine and heroin manufactured in illicit labs nestled along the Burmese-Thai borders.

I was horrified when Dr. Sukett told me that the presence of the American military in South Vietnam had created an increase in demand for making opium into heroin. The United States used Thailand for "R and R" furloughs for their troops and too many of the military were eager to try these easily accessible drugs. Our government also aided in the distribution of opium by building a network of highways in Northern Thailand to facilitate the movement of the US military stationed there. Now it was easy to transport opium shipments.

As our trucks traveled cautiously around curves and up the steep road, I noticed that many of the hillsides had large ugly burned areas stripped of all vegetation. Dr. Sukett pointed out that this was the result of the "slash and burn" method used by the farmers. When they had grown three or four crops of poppies and the soil was depleted, they merely choose another area, slashed down the trees and shrubs, set it afire and prepared the ground for their next crop. As a result the forests of Northern Thailand were being destroyed.

Finally, our trucks pulled carefully over to the edge of the narrow dirt road and stopped. The view across the valleys and mountains was exquisite: a patchwork of colors which included large fields of red poppies, yellow squares where crops had been harvested, and the dark brown slash and burn sections. Just below us about one hundred feet down a steep slope, we saw a tribal woman harvesting an opium crop with two small children clinging to her skirts. To observe more closely we had to tread carefully down the steep hillside to keep from sliding and trampling the plants.

Woman harvesting opium

I was overcome with a feeling of despair as I watched this woman, probably in her early twenties, working out in the full sun on such a hot, humid day. She looked weary and her drawn face, lifeless hair, and shabby clothes made her seem very, very old. I wanted to cry for her children, who clutched her skirt and played in the dirt at her feet. They, too, looked weary with their sad faces, tattered clothes, and undernourished bodies. The sorrow in this mother's eyes continues to haunt me to this day.

Their home at the edge of the field was a mere platform with bamboo walls on three sides and a thatched roof. I saw only a few pots, some rags which were used for blankets and nothing of the amenities of life. I shivered as I thought how cold the evening would be for them and was ashamed that I had looked forward to this trip as only an exciting adventure. I thought of the contrast between the lives of these simple folk who were growing the opium and the opulent lives of those who sold it in my country. The contrast between this shack and our drug mansions was overwhelming.

One of my Thai friends explained that this woman was using a tool with three sharp prongs which incised the side of the poppy pod in three places. Soon the thick, sticky, dark opium oozed through these cuts and the woman later returned with a wooden pallet and scraped the substance off onto a large flat banana leaf which she balanced on her forearm. When she had a sizable ball, it was rolled up and lain aside. These leaf packages of opium were easy to transport because they didn't spoil. In fact, one could bury them in the ground and come back a few years later to find them unchanged. These would soon be ready for collection and carried off the mountain on the back of a horse or mule to be made into heroin or exported around the world.

I was shocked again when Dr. Sukett told me that this was not a good growing year and so this family would earn only about seventy American dollars for their crop. Since they had not learned to grow anything else and must therefore purchase all of their food in a marketplace, it was no wonder they looked undernourished and hungry.

On the ride back to Baw Gao, as I expressed my dismay at these conditions, my Thai companions told me about the many projects, both Thai and international, that were trying to improve the life of these people. Kasetsart University of Thailand was working nearby to introduce cash crops ranging from subtropical fruit trees and cut flowers, to vegetables and ornamental plants, aimed at curbing further destruction of forests and weaning the tribal people from planting more opium. They tried to teach the people they could earn more in a shorter period and use less tilled land with these new crops. At first the farmers were distrustful and it was taking a long process of education before they would try something new. Now, however, along with the free transportation of their crops to market, some were asking for more of the free seeds and fertilizers. which these programs provided along with rice well below the market price.

The ride back to Chiang Mai was even more strenuous for we were all tired. This time the girls were not able to wait until the truck stopped and paper bags were used liberally as we swung around the mountain roads. No time for talking. One student nurse even had to be left at the hospital overnight because she had become so dehydrated.

That afternoon as we bumped along in the dust and heat I was overwhelmed by many emotions. There was a feeling of weariness and depression after having witnessed such a desperate way of life, but also there was the elation of working with and seeing this international medical team serving people in need. No one preached a sermon or quoted scripture during the trip. A group of strangers started out to the mountains, worked and sweat together, walked, laughed, and enjoyed the beauty of the earth—ministering "unto the least of these my brethren." Up there in the mountains I had been privileged to see the healing of bodies and souls.

ELEPHANT ISLAND

Back in the comfort of my Chiang Mai apartment and once more immersed in the everyday routine of school, it was difficult to imagine that the hard lives I had witnessed for only a short time up there in the mountains had been anything but a dream—but more doses of reality were to come.

When I had first arrived and found the international community so involved in various interesting humanitarian projects, I had put out the word that I would love to be included on any expedition in which there was a spare seat. I must have passed muster this past weekend because already I was being invited to another place of great interest to me—the McKean Leprosy Hospital.

Leprosy, for me, had always conjured images of hideously malformed people sitting in squalor as they begged for alms and food outside the gates of an ancient city. I suppose I first heard of the dreaded flesh eating disease in Sunday school when the Bible talked about those "unclean" creatures whom no one wanted to be near, let alone touch. Leprosy was considered loathsome and completely incurable, with the victims in more recent times being banished to colonies where there was no fear of others being contaminated. I must admit to feeling a sense of apprehension at the thought of myself walking among such people but I gave the invitation an enthusiastic, "Yes!"

That is how early the next Thursday morning found me on my way to the famous McKean Leprosy Hospital located 8 km down river from Chiang Mai. I was in a VW bug driven by Dottie. She and her husband Bob were agriculture missionaries. The previous week after the International Church service, Bob insisted, with a twinkle in his eye, that I join them with other friends, for dinner at an "authentic" Thai restaurant. When it came time to order, Bob took over because "he knew the best items on the menu!" The main dish was soon dramatically set right in front of me. Knowing Bob's sense of humor, I immediately became suspicious. "What is this, Bob?" I inquired. "Just goat stew," he replied. I looked more critically at the contents and it didn't take me long to realize that all body parts were included in the stew. Staring up at me were eyeballs and floating next to them—were teats. I didn't delve any deeper, afraid of what else I would find. Bob and the group had a good laugh at me as I carefully spooned out a few pieces of honest to goodness goat meat.

Now they were on their way to hold their regular Bible study for the agricultural workers on the island. As Dottie maneuvered her dusty vehicle around potholes and debris, down the narrow two lane road made into a tunnel by the bamboo and rain forest trees arching overhead, she shared the unusual story of how an elephant and a powerful prince of the Lannathai Kingdom were instrumental in the realization of this hospital.

In 1897 Dr. James W. McKean, a Presbyterian medical missionary, arrived in Chiang Mai and started a Medical clinic to help the many sick people around the city. It wasn't long before he became deeply concerned about the plight of the lepers whom he saw wandering about begging or coming to his clinic for alms and medicine. Finding that their requests met with a sympathetic, practical response, they began to come in increasing numbers and frequency.

Overwhelmed by their need, Dr. McKean repeatedly appealed to the Bangkok government for help but it wasn't until 1908 that things began to happen. It came about in a strange way. Dr. McKean was personal physician to the ruling Prince of Chiang Mai. When the Prince's eldest son came of age, his father gave him a "good luck" present of an enormous white elephant, but it proved to be a vicious creature, killing its keepers and becoming too dangerous to keep. Wondering what to do with him, someone came up with the idea of hobbling his front legs with heavy chains and banishing him to an island south of the city. The great beast soon became master of the 160 acres which he ruled with great vigor, destroying the island village and tearing down granaries and houses to obtain food. Finally the villagers fled and he remained the sole occupant until his death.

The young prince, also Dr. McKean's patient, eventually succeeded his father as Prince of Chiang Mai. Being a generous man, upon request he gave the elephant's island to Dr. McKean.

Now the Doctor was the owner of a large piece of property but it was overgrown with briars and thorns and he had no funds to even purchase clothes and food for the nine leprosy patients anxious to take up residence. It was hardly an auspicious beginning for the hospital of his dreams, but he forged ahead and with hard work the jungle was cleared, rough huts were erected, and the care of patients begun.

Soon we rattled across the covered wooden bridge Dr. McKean had built over a branch of the Ping River and continued through a few more miles of jungle before the road broke out into farmland. We passed between mango and lumyai orchards and cultivated fields dotted with lovely old Thai houses, then finally stopped at a tractor shed where twenty men and women quietly waited, seated on wooden benches and mats on the floor. I knew that all of them were either patients, ex-patients, or family of patients, and although I felt them watching me as I climbed out of the small car, I was reluctant to look at them; afraid of what I might see and of not being able to hide my shock. Carefully I gathered my belongings and finally, having run out of excuses, I faced the group. Dottie introduced me and they all politely nodded. Maybe there was a scar or two, one man had a wooden leg, but I saw nothing terrible at all! I smiled back and happily accepted a seat among them.

First we sang hymns from a hymnal with Thai words and music, then Dottie taught from the study book. It was the same lesson that was being used at all five services being held at the same time across the island. I had been told that, although not all the people were Christians, all were expected to attend.

After the class, Bob talked with his Thai boss and discussed the work for the day. The men and women then left to go to their different farming assignments. They and others like them were responsible for all the crops on the island. Bob was anxious to make the farm self sufficient, so the profits could be used to support the farmers' families and pay for the equipment and buildings. The most important goal, however, was to build self-esteem among a severely stigmatized people.

We drove over to the administration office where I learned more about this hospital now called the McKean Rehabilitation Center. This name change was effected because, due to the discovery in 1947 of the sulphone drug Dapsone and other medical advances, they were now able to concentrate more on rehabilitation than treatment. For most Thais however, the word leprosy, now called Hanson's disease, struck terror into their very souls and the doctors were having an uphill fight against fear and ignorance to get them to understand that early diagnosis was essential to prevent progression and crippling.

Most people in the world have a natural, complete resistance against this mildly contagious disease spread by a germ resembling the one which causes T.B. However, malnutrition, debilitating illness and bad sanitation could weaken this protection, so for the vulnerable and superstitious poor, a "skin" clinic had been set up in Chiang Mai. Here folk came for other problems and while treating them the Doctors could keep a secret lookout for signs of leprosy.

I was happily surprised to learn that my Alma Mater, the University of Illinois, had been conducting research with McKean doctors for several years. This knowledge forged a connection for me with this inspiring place and made me feel more than just a casual guest.

We got back into the bug and toured the island—so green and fertile, it was hard to imagine it covered with brush and ruled by one angry elephant! A breeze from the river eased the noontime heat and swayed the branches of the 300 coconut palms.

We stopped at a whitewashed, screened building to visit men and women who had recently undergone surgery. Unfortunately many deformities occurred before the patients got here, but the doctors did an amazing job of reconstructing muscles which had been paralyzed due to nerve damage, or making cosmetic repairs which give the patient the self-confidence to reenter society. They seemed happy, smiling at us through their facial bandages or waving wrapped arms.

We moved on to watch as patients in another cottage had their hands massaged or did exercises prescribed by the resident physiotherapist. In a well furnished prosthetic workshop, a former leprosy patient used his misshapened fingers to carefully make a pair of special shoes to protect the feet in which he had lost all feeling, and an amputee proudly showed us the two legs he was making: one wooden peg leg to wear while working in the fields and another more sophisticated version to wear in public.

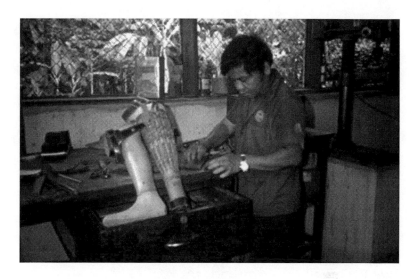

Man making leg

All over the compound patients worked industriously. I had previously heard about the wonderful teak furniture made here and now admired the intricate carving being done on tables, chairs and cabinets. I promised myself I would return soon and buy two silverware chests for my children. The workers beamed at my obvious admiration and I wandered on to watch the tedious art of lacquerware. Others using stencils made Christmas cards. Women were weaving, making baskets, sewing and doing delicate stitchery on small tablecloths and napkins, all the while chattering cheerfully to each other. As large ceiling fans circulated the air in this pleasant, creative place, I lost the last of any preconceived ideas I had had about leprosy. From now on whenever that disease was mentioned I would remember these happy faces and the miracle of restored bodies.

I asked Dottie how long the patients stayed here. In the past, she told me, they were kept on the island for life but two problems arose: when treatment stopped the symptoms, many patients wanted to go home and back to work, also, the island became overcrowded. After much thought there emerged a plan for Rehabilitation Villages to care for those who were not accepted back by their families or villages. Every ten people who would train in the treatment of leprosy, were given land and a bamboo house and allowed to start a new village where the resident patients were encouraged to make it on their own. Already seventeen such communities in Northern Thailand were visited once a month by a medical team which provided follow-up treatment and help with self-supporting skills.

Toward the end of our visit we walked down a narrow street bordered by small, private homes inhabited by the permanently crippled, blind, or deaf. They were allowed to stay for life. When I asked about the pots hanging by each gate, my attention was directed to the ox drawn cart which was at that moment lumbering down the street. It came from the main kitchen and I watched as food was carefully placed in each pot for the main meal.

It was time to leave and as we drove through the farmland with its many heavily laden fruit trees and fields of healthy looking vegetables, I looked back at what appeared to be nothing other than an attractive, well cared for Thai village. Then the jungle swallowed us and we clattered back across the bridge to the mainland.

In the year before my visit, over 2,000 leprosy patients had been treated at McKean and four hundred operations performed. Each year the number of new cases declines as the education process takes hold and the disease is diagnosed earlier. Now there is even a school on the island for children to attend while they are being treated. "Early diagnosis—Early cure" is the McKean slogan.

I left "Elephant Island" that day with a deep feeling of respect for the long ago Presbyterian doctor who had persevered until he made his dream come true. Because of one man's concern for these "unclean" people, Northern Thailand was a much healthier place and a dreaded disease was on the decline.

A BUDDHIST CHRISTMAS?

Christmas approached and I faced it with trepidation. A Buddhist country certainly wouldn't celebrate this, my favorite holiday. My children would be far away and I with my choir background would sorely miss the familiar Christmas music. What about the seasonal traditions I had always honored? Would I end up sitting alone in my room listening to the tapes of carols my friends had pressed upon me before I left the States? I braced myself to face disappointment in this country where less than half of one percent of the population was Christian.

Letters began arriving with promises of prayers for me during the holiday and it was obvious that my distant friends also thought I would be lonely and homesick. Mark and Lorie sent me tapes so I would be certain to hear their voices as there was no guarantee of Thailand's unpredictable telephone service being able to connect us on that important day.

The first sign that my presumptions might be wrong came one day in early November as I shopped in Chiang Mai. I was concentrating on picking out some melons in the market when a sound insinuated itself on my subconscious. It filtered through the general hubbub, demanding my attention, but for a time I ignored it. Suddenly I stopped and listened—it was Bing Crosby singing, "I'm Dreaming of a White Christmas". I couldn't believe my ears! How incongruous the words sounded in this bustling tropical market so far from home, but how wonderful!

That same week many of the primary teachers at my Thai school asked me to come to their classrooms to teach Christmas songs to their students. I must have taught thirty to forty classes how to sing "Jingle Bells," "Silent Night," and their favorite, "White Christmas."

My calendar began to fill with amazing speed: Payap University Christmas Concert, parties at both schools where I taught, Open Houses, Christmas Eve dinner, Church services, midnight supper on Christmas Eve, dinner invitation for Christmas Day, and finally the parade at the McKean Rehabilitation Center on Christmas night. At this rate I would find little time to listen to my own tapes—this festive time might not be so bad after all!

In fact the Christmas Concert at Payap University set the stage for one of the most exciting Christmases I've ever experienced. This Christian University in Chiang Mai had the most outstanding music department of any school in Thailand and the young people were so amazingly talented I still get goose bumps remembering their choral groups singing traditional Christmas music in both Thai and English. Their program included string ensembles, recorder groups, and a bell choir in addition to the choral numbers. Somehow the old favorite carols and hymns took on new meaning when sung in a different language and I found myself listening to them more carefully and gaining new understanding.

There were no days off for Christmas in the Thai community, but since Dara was a Christian school the 25th was a holiday. When I came in on the 24th the campus was transformed. A prize was to be awarded for the classroom best decorated in the theme of the Christ Child's birth. Each class had tried to outdo the others. Desks were pushed aside and there was a lot of straw as the girls had built actual mangers.

I went from room to room looking and exclaiming. They were all beautiful but the prize went to the group who had pushed all their desks into the center of the room to resemble a stage. Girls wearing Biblical costumes made out of large Turkish towels and blankets, formed a tableau on top of the straw-covered desks. They were the Wise Men, shepherds, angels, Mary and Joseph—and two girls covered in white sheets were the sheep! A lovely dark-skinned baby Jesus doll lay sleeping in a straw-filled manger. No lights were on, only candles flickered as one student stood quietly in the corner of the room playing "Silent Night" on a flute while the rest of the class, hidden under the desks, softly sang along.

Christmas at Dara

The beauty of it brought tears to my eyes. Here all the props were handmade. The paper chains that hung from the ceiling were formed from old newspapers, not the expensive, colored construction paper used by my classes in the States, yet they were just as lovely. The creativity and talent of these young girls, using only materials at hand, made the manger scene more real to me. Their interpretation of the first Christmas seemed more fitting than any of the glamorous, commercial ones I remembered at home. I was beginning to like my Thai Christmas.

After viewing the decorated room, Ahjahn Perla greeted me and ushered me into each of the classrooms where I taught. Thai girls are very enthusiastic and scream and giggle with little provocation, so I was met with screams and greetings in each room. The head girl gave a speech dedicated to Acharn Jackie and presented me with a gift. I was overwhelmed. I had been told that teachers in Thailand were held in high esteem and was finding this to be true with each new experience. I received beautiful large hand-painted fans, a Thai skirt, blouses, ceramic animals, two reed bags, a reed plant holder, and purses. In fact I received so many gifts I had to hire a samlaw to carry my treasures home. And indeed these were treasures for these girls were so warm I knew each gift was truly from the heart. I was then embarrassed to receive gifts from each teacher in the English department. Fortunately the Thais made a big celebration of the New Year, so I could reciprocate at the end of the week without looking too foolish.

There were more services offered than I could possibly attend. I was especially anxious to worship in the Thai Presbyterian Church on the Sunday before Christmas. They had many choirs and special music, with the children included in the first half of the service. Then their Sunday School teachers came out with baskets of Christmas decorations that the children had made to be given to the members of the congregation. I noticed that some of the teachers had to encourage the children to give their decorations away. One delightful small boy who clutched five of them in his chubby hand seemed not at all sure about this "joy of giving" experience.

After the service I watched the party put on by the Sunday School classes for children from the Chiang Mai slums. I was greatly impressed by the many teenagers who graciously directed the games and then served the bountiful meal. After the last plate was scraped clean the guests went home with full tummies and a large bag of candy, biscuits, and fruit.

Hating to miss anything, I attended three church services on Christmas Eve. First was the service at the International Church, which was in English. Next I went to the Thai church to participate in a traditional Thai Christian service, and finally I hurried over to the Anglican Midnight Service as I always attended a midnight service at my home church.

Before attending all these services I had prepared Christmas Eve dinner for ten people in my apartment. Since I had always had friends in my home on Christmas Eve in California, especially international students from our local seminaries, I continued this tradition by inviting my Chiang Mai friends—all from the states, but also far from home. As I did at my Moraga Christmas party, I asked everyone to tell where they were from and to share news about their family and Christmas traditions. This time we heard about Christmas in Ohio, Texas, Nebraska, Pennsylvania, and California. I fell into bed very late that night, exhausted, but with a heart brimful of holiday spirit.

On Christmas morning all of us in Ding-a-ling dorm, as we had been christened, had breakfast together and opened our gifts. I served my special Fridell family recipe of creamed eggs on muffins. They didn't taste quite the same with ingredients bought in Chiang Mai but it was another good time with new friends.

Later we were all invited to Christmas dinner at the home of a co-worker who had lived in Chiang Mai for twenty-three years and had her own house. It was filled with beautiful Christmas decorations and her excellent cook served us baked ham, sweet potatoes in orange cups, broccoli, cole slaw, a Thai cranberry relish, bread and butter pickles, and mincemeat pie. It was all delicious and as good as any Christmas dinner I'd ever had.

That night we went out to the McKean Rehabilitation Center to see one of the annual highlights of the Chiang Mai Christmas season, the Candlelight Parade. The floats were each decorated by a different McKean department and each was preceded by a large group of marchers carrying colorful Thai lanterns. Again I was impressed at how such beauty had been created from the humblest of origins and how proud these leprosy patients were of their accomplishments. The parade led the way to the McKean Chapel for Christmas worship, and as we stood in the crowded church, I was moved by the sound of voices raised in thanks, and the joy shining from the faces around me.

To be truthful I had felt a few pangs of homesickness at the thought of my children and family being so far away. New friends, however, kept me smiling and the simple, humble way the Thai Christians celebrated added special meaning and appreciation to that miracle in Bethlehem. I missed being home with my family, but a Thai Christmas definitely had its own special rewards and blessings.

TO BURMA WITH LOVE

Ed and Norma were not very explicit about where we were going, but they had invited me to join them on a five-day trip to the western border of Thailand. I couldn't believe my luck that all these hardworking missionaries could be bothered to include me on their busy and often demanding journeys. The more I saw of them, the more I realized how truly dedicated they were to helping others, not forcing their religious beliefs on them. They were the antithesis of the culture-destroying missionaries of Michner's *Hawaii* and I greatly admired their empathy for people of every race and level, in any situation, with complete disregard for their own wealth or comfort. And yet they were still very human—they joked, played guitars, argued and got angry, made mistakes, and rejoiced at their successes. I arranged for a few days off from school and gathered what I was told to bring: a sleeping bag, mosquito netting, a "phasin" and casual clothes. I must admit I raised my eyebrows about the phasin, a tube of Thai cotton which I was told I would need when bathing in a river!

When the Toyoto pickup arrived it was already loaded with food, literature, supplies, and several Karens who were hitching a ride. Transportation to remote areas was very limited, so it was rare to see missionaries traveling without a number of passengers. The air-conditioning and tape deck may have seemed luxury items but definitely were not—a ten-hour drive in the tropics in the hot season over unpaved roads with all the windows up against the dust, is a challenge. A tape deck with therapeutic music is a must in a country where Thais make California drivers look like saints. I squeezed myself and my belongings in and we were off.

We stopped late that first afternoon beside the Moei River at Mae Sot, another bustling little village like all the others we had passed on our ten-hour drive. With Burma on the opposite bank, this was where the majority of black market goods such as calculators, wristwatches, tape recorders, cameras, and medicine, along with an array of household items, were smuggled over the Thai border to be sold in Rangoon. From Burma, smugglers returned with teak, ivory, jade, and other precious stones.

I watched, fascinated by the constant parade of people who walked back and forth across the narrow plank bridge that connected Thailand to Burma. Since the little shops in the village were loaded with Thai textiles, I was not surprised to see bolts of material being carried on heads and shoulders. Bicycles, mysterious unmarked boxes, and food moved in a continuous stream.

I wondered why but didn't ask, when we stopped to pick up more supplies from the market to pack into our already overloaded pickup. Then we headed south of Mae Sot to spend the night in the small Thai village of Morichai with Pastor Nupaw. This delightful gentleman had been born in Burma where he became a Christian, then attended seminary in Rangoon, and finally migrated to Thailand to work as a Karen pastor. He had been attending seminars in Chiang Mai for the past three weeks and was now to be with his wife and three children for one night, then off again for another three weeks to serve his allocation of churches.

Soon after our arrival, we were led down to the river to bathe. I was not very adept at using my phasin and the Karen children watching me from the bank obviously thought my antics hilarious. First I pulled the material over my head and with a struggle undressed inside it before stepping into the river. I was amazed and delighted by the warm, clear water and had no qualms about bathing there, something I would never consider near the developed areas with their polluted streams. Contented, I relaxed in one of the most refreshing baths I had ever had.

Refreshing river bath with audience

But now came the challenge of dressing with my giggly audience still watching. I must cover myself with a dry phasin, at the same time dropping the wet one to the ground and then dressing, while staying discretely covered—one of my greatest challenges since arriving in Thailand!

Walking back to the bamboo house where we were to spend the night, I realized that Pastor Nupaw's family lived in a well-stocked pantry. Within a short distance I passed coffee plants, tea, bananas, coconut palms, betel nuts, mango, papaya, pomelo, limes, countless vegetables and herbs, and a menagerie of goats, oxen, chickens, pigs, and ducks. I noticed the area around the house had obviously been carefully swept in anticipation of father returning home with farang visitors.

Before we had left for the river, Norma had unloaded some goodies from the truck; several loaves of her delicious homemade bread and peanut butter, and the vegetables and meat purchased in the market at Mae Sot. Now I understood the last minute shopping and realized she probably spent a considerable amount of time before each trip, trying to anticipate how many different homes she would visit so was sure to have plenty of food to share in each. A delicious Karen meal was ready for us. It included rice, cooked vegetables, three meat dishes (in honor of the farangs) and the most delicious curried fish I had ever eaten. Bananas and oranges were served for dessert and we drank "boiled cold water" specially prepared for us. Then Ed was asked to preach that night.

After dinner a bell began to ring and we carefully stepped over a wooden stile into the church yard. Ed quickly jotted down some notes, the pastor unlocked the church door and soon the congregation began to gather. I was amazed to see over fifty people carrying hymnals quietly arrive within twenty minutes for an unscheduled worship service.

Ed was careful to sit at the side of the church, insisting that the pastor occupy the seat in front of the congregation. Norma explained that it was important that the pastor not be usurped by the missionary or that his status as leader be threatened. The missionary was only there to assist.

After the service many families returned to the Nupaws' home as Ed and Norma had brought a box of children's sweaters donated by friends in America. The youngsters waited patiently for someone to hand them their warm gift. There was no grabbing or exchanging, just grateful smiles and quiet acceptance.

Many stayed on to watch Pastor Nupaw fill out and sign the papers for the Rice Bank which the village would soon build and for which Ed had brought money for the initial purchase of the grain. We talked into the night.

. . . and again I had to listen to dear missionary friends rave about my father-in-law who years before had been responsible for their being commissioned as missionaries here in Thailand. They were all special people whom I admired so very much for their caring and concern.

But again, they dredged up the memories of Lee and his depression. From as far back as he could remember, Lee had been told by his mother to "look up to your father and be like him." It wasn't until Lee was in serious therapy that his real feelings emerged. This was again a most painful experience. He had spent his life trying to be like his father and yet had never received any recognition from him.

*Lee's grandfather was a minister, his father was a minister, even his brother was a minister/missionary. But Lee was only a teacher. A VERY GOOD teacher. He chose **not** to be a minister and compete with the rest. But, this was never appreciated. During therapy he realized the pain he carried from having been denied love and admiration from his father. He also became aware of the way his father solicited praise and admiration from any group he was in, always being the center of attention. For Lee, in his mid-fifties, to realize that the man he tried to emulate, was not the person he wanted to admire—was devastating.*

Once when Lee had taken a leave from his teaching, because of his depression, he unwisely chose to take off to visit his parents, still searching for recognition. I discouraged his going, but he was adamant. When he arrived by train that evening and was picked up by his parents, he tried to tell them he was in depression, suffering, and in great pain. When he said, "Dad, I'm really hurting and need to talk to you about it"—his father changed the subject and replied, "Oh, look! There's our new stadium."

Lee fell apart that night, called his brother who lived in the same town and walked out of his parents' home. I was phoned in the middle of the night and drove five hours to pick him up and bring him home. This was the final blow for reaching out to his Dad. He never tried again.

The next morning Ed took me to see the potential site for the Rice Bank and explained what a boon this would be to the village. People would be able to "deposit" rice when it was in abundance and "borrow" in time of need without having to pay the usual 50 to 100 percent interest. This was a popular program in Thailand but it was often hard for a community to find the funds for such a project.

In mid-afternoon we headed off again in the Toyota. After an uneventful few miles on narrow, dusty roads we rounded a corner to be faced by a group of armed soldiers standing by a guard house. They motioned for us to stop and Ed got out and walked toward them. I glanced at Norma but although she watched intently she didn't appear to be nervous. I licked my dry lips but said nothing and we waited in quiet as the men talked. Finally Ed returned with a big grin on his face and without a word we continued on our way.

I was bursting to know what had happened and finally Ed told me that we had just been given permission to cross the border into Burma. Having neither passports nor visas seemed to be no problem in this remote border area, but now I realized why I had not been told of our destination. These things were done very quietly.

Ed and Norma worked with the estimated 400,000 Karen tribal people of Northern and Western Thailand. However there were another six million across the border in Burma.

Those who lived on the Burma/Thailand border had been at war with the Burmese government ever since Burma had gained independence from Britain in 1952. The Karens felt unfairly treated by the ruling Buddhist Burmese who had failed to pass on the same freedom they had acquired as promised and instead fought against any ethnic minority that requested its own autonomy. This was another reason for not publicizing our visit, because we were here to attend a meeting of the Burmese Karen Baptists, gathered for their annual conference on the border. Fighting was only 50 kilometers away. We must be careful.

Soon we arrived at the village where the conference was being held and were directed to our quarters in an old army barracks.

On our way to our assigned rooms, we passed a table where a Karen army officer in camouflage fatigues sat with his machine gun propped against the wall and a short-wave radio in front of him. This gentleman was in contact with the fighting units up the road and would keep us informed as to their activities. Because we were farangs, we were given the "deluxe quarters" where we spread our sleeping bags on the wooden floors and hung mosquito netting over the uncovered windows. The 700 Karens who attended the conference would sleep out in the open.

These people had all walked or traveled in the back of trucks, one of which we watched roll in with approximately fifty people in it, all standing, as that was the only way they would fit. They had ridden for several hours this way over hot, dusty mountain roads and reported seeing one crowded truck slide off at a bad curve. But no problem, everyone simply hopped off as it slid, pushed it back up and so arrived only a little late.

A large flat area had been cleared next to a small church on the top of a hill. The ground was covered with a flat bamboo roof for shade and under it straw was spread for the Karens to sit on.

The theme of the conference was Psalm 46:1, "The Lord is my refuge and strength. A very present help in time of trouble." This was especially meaningful as so many had family members fighting in the war just a few miles away.

During the seventeen meetings I attended, many things impressed me; the number of women used in positions of leadership in a part of the world that does not usually honor women's participation; the number of children who sat quietly on the ground for hours; the instant, spontaneous singing and the twenty choirs who took turns entertaining us and who seemed to have an endless supply of songs. Amazing, too, were the fifteen people ranging in age from 10 to 70 who stood and recited 50 verses of scripture in unison without stopping. But best of all was the friendly, happy, spirited feeling that emanated from this assembly of devout people.

Following one three-hour morning service, Ed was asked to baptize eleven young people in their late teens. Spectators in colorful red and blue Karen outfits crowded both banks of a narrow stream closed in by the dense rain forest. This provided a beautiful back drop as the six boys and five girls, dressed in white robes, were led into the stream and reverently immersed.

Out of concern for those fighting, a 24-hour fast was planned. But first, following the Baptism, we were led to a dining area where planks were laden with dishes of rice and vegetables. This was our final meal until the next afternoon. An all night prayer vigil for peace was held on the top of the hill and it was a rare experience to sit under the stars in this remote area of Burma while the Karens around us prayed for their army and their enemies. As I sat with these new friends, I was reminded that these Karen men were fighting for their independence and freedom just as our forefathers had done in America 200 years before. I felt a great sense of awe at being able to share this precious time with these troubled people.

My trip to Burma was one of the most meaningful adventures I had while living in Thailand. Not understanding the Karen language, I spent much of my time during those days observing, not talking. I cherished being with these stalwart tribal folk who showed such gentle strength in their every day existence. They persevered. They cared. They hurt. They were trying to find hope and improve their displaced lives under very adverse refugee conditions. I sensed and knew all these things without our sharing a word.

MY THAIS

"Be a good listener and don't expect to make close friends of the Thai people." These were the two directives I remembered most from the orientation I had attended in New York before heading for Thailand. Since I had the reputation of being a big talker, I knew I would have difficulty curbing my tongue and since I enjoyed making new friends, I was disappointed to think I would not get to know the Thais. They are a "private" people, we were told.

During my first few weeks I had enjoyed many parties and had occasion to meet many of the international community. The city was full of interesting workers from around the world who had come to help this Northern area of Thailand which was taking longer to develop because of its inaccessibility. At any dinner party I could sit and hear about someone's work with the World Bank, learn about soil conservation, reforestation, new surgery techniques for lepers or the latest work being done with tribal languages. This was all very interesting but I longed to know the Thai people. I was eager to experience and be accepted as part of their community.

This is why I was so thrilled when Bonjob, our Thai school custodian, invited me to attend the 100 day anniversary of the death of his father. This was originally a Buddhist custom but Thai Christians had maintained the practice and simply changed the service to a Christian one. I was one of five farangs in a group of about sixty and it was like any family party. We gathered on the lawn of Bonjob's home where tables covered with colorful Thai delicacies were set up under the trees. For the service we sat comfortably on wooden folding chairs, which was a real treat for me after my many agonizing experiences of sitting on wooden floors with my feet tucked under me. The service was in Thai, but although I did not comprehend each word, I felt at ease and hoped that this was a good start toward my goal of making Thai friends.

Next my neighbor, Donna, and I jumped at the chance to attend a Buddhist festival in the village of Chunsom, our cook. It was a small place typical of the area, and since it was about five miles north of Chiang Mai, most of the inhabitants worked as laborers in the city. Each night they returned to their wood framed, thatched houses most of which had one or two open rooms with a minimum of furniture; usually a table and possibly a chair or two. Mats always covered the floor for the family to sit on for meals and sleep on at night.

Since we were the only farangs in the village that evening, we were treated as honored guests which was rather embarrassing but we had no choice other than to accept their warm hospitality. Chunsom had fixed a light dinner of barbecued pork rind, chicken with a cucumber sauce, and sticky rice, which we enjoyed with the family while sitting on the floor. She had also asked her niece, who spoke a little English, to join us and help explain things.

After dinner we joined the members of the village who were gathering to walk to the Wat. Each ceremoniously bore a gift for the monks, one means of earning merit for their afterlife. These offerings were tied to small stripped branches from a tree and carried aloft like flags. I was aware that the Buddhist monks and students had no money and everything they needed was supplied by the members of their Wat, so when I saw branches decorated with food, towels, baskets, even folding chairs, I wondered if the monks had a "wish list" which they passed out ahead of time for the things they needed.

The procession was preceded by a marching band of about six men with percussion instruments and a couple of flute-like pipes. Behind them, dancing and singing, came the followers carrying candles. To me it was pure magic to see the flickering lights and joyous people winding up the road on this balmy peaceful evening so far from the hectic rush of the modern world.

When we arrived at the Wat, fireworks were set off and dancing commenced in the courtyard. The petite Thai women looked lovely with their printed cotton sarongs wrapped around their waists; little girls in brightly colored stoles skipped and twirled so their full skirts flared and the men were handsome in the traditional loose shirt with its high stiff collar.

When the last and largest group arrived, one older gentleman did a sword dance which got faster and faster as the drums kept time to his steps. Hands clapped frantically until he finally pretended to drive a sword into his stomach and fell to the ground apparently mortally wounded. It was **very** convincing to me and I was enormously relieved when he finally stood up and bowed with dignity to the cheers of the crowd.

Later that evening riding back through the countryside to Chiang Mai in a bicycle taxi, I struggled to hide my nervousness, for there were many strange sounds and no lights. The night seemed completely black as towering bamboo hovered overhead shutting out the moon and stars. I could see no evidence of a road but put my faith in Buen Luen, our cook's husband, an experienced samlor driver, and we did get quickly and safely home.

It was good to have been with Thais in their own Thai village sharing their joyous festival and I went to sleep feeling very happy.

My desk at Dara Academy was in an office with six Thai teachers and we had many good times together. Often they asked questions about where I lived in Chiang Mai and what my place was like so I decided to have them over Saturday and give them a typical "farang lunch." I chose to serve chicken salad because they were familiar with all the ingredients and I didn't want to shock them with something too strange the first time they came. My salad consisted of chicken, green grapes, pineapple, nuts, lettuce and a curry dressing. I also baked cinnamon rolls not too different from some of the pastries found in the market.

I decided to serve them at a table on my porch and set it just as I would at home with a knife, fork, and teaspoon at each place. After borrowing enough chairs I was ready for my guests and fervently hoped the silverware wouldn't be too much of a problem as they were used to having only a tablespoon. Thais seldom used a knife as most of their food was already cut up while larger pieces are eaten with fingers.

My Thai teacher friends

My ladies arrived and sat down. I served the food and they laughed and giggled as they tried to eat the salad with a fork while I instructed. The cinnamon rolls were a big hit and all were eager to learn how to make them, so I promised a baking lesson in the near future. By the end of our party I was feeling good about our relationship and decided it wasn't going to be at all hard to make friends with these delightful co-workers.

The group left and Chunsom and I began to clear things away. She beckoned for me to look under the table. There were most of the grapes, plus pieces of chicken, lettuce, and pineapple. Evidently the forks had proved too much.

Since Dara Academy was a private school with a small tuition, most of the girls came from middle to upper middle class families. Supit, a Mauteum Hah student, and I began to have a special relationship. She was the youngest of ten children and had lost her mother to rheumatic fever several years earlier. She told me how her father, who was a teacher, had raised the eight girls and two boys with the aim that every child in the family would get a college education—a great accomplishment in this country.

Supit was a very out-going young lady, quick to smile and always ready for fun. While many of my students treated me with caution, Supit seemed to feel at ease with this farang teacher. She was an outstanding student: in addition to being head of the Christian Club, she played the trombone in the school band, was a champion badminton player and a goalie in soccer. As her sister was a teacher at Dara, the two felt comfortable inviting me to their homes.

Supit's was a typical, beautiful old teak house. It was large, with big open rooms, and as usual very little furniture. In the different homes I visited in Thailand, there was seldom any sense of "decorating" as we do in America. Our homes are filled with pictures, knickknacks, books, extra furniture and plants. Their homes were uncluttered and exuded tranquility. I decided that with ten children to raise, paying for a good education must take priority over possessions. However, even where there was evidence of plenty of money in a family, homes were kept simple. What you would always find, however, were family pictures and this was especially true here with a family of ten children.

After visiting in Supit's home, she took me across town to the home of her sister on the army base where her handsome husband was a Captain. He had completed the Thai "West Point" academy and would soon be off to Bangkok for a year of special training as he moved up the military ladder. He was following in the footsteps of his father and brother who were also keen military men. What an ambitious and wonderful people these were!

The picture changed however. A few months before I left Thailand. Supit came to my home and told a very different story. Up to this time she had always spoken of a caring father who supported and encouraged his children, but now she told of how her father had left home many years ago to enjoy a second wife, not an unusual situation in Thailand. He had moved out while her mother was still sick causing much grief and had not supported the education of his children. Supit tearfully admitted that if she wanted to go to college she must do it on her own. For the first time I was hearing a sad, personal story from a Thai and my heart went out to her. I became a "Mom" to Supit and in the years to come I followed her through college, and adopted her and her husband when they came to the states for several years. I became "grandmother" to her two sons and they spent many happy times in our home. Here I found the warm, caring, intimate relationship I had sought.

I looked forward to my first dinner at the home of Acharn Somsri, the School Manager. A Manager was in charge of the Academy, and under her "head teachers", whom we would call principals, were responsible for the elementary, junior high, and high schools. Somsri was considered one of the top educators in Thailand, but I like to think of her as an "ordinary" great person. Neither dress, manner, nor conversation readily revealed her fine mind, and her understanding of modern education. While she had done her undergraduate work in Thailand, all of her graduate studies were completed in the United States, and because of this she was very accepting of this energetic, outspoken foreigner at her school.

It had taken me a while to figure out the dress code for various occasions in this culture. I seemed to have overdressed every time I had gone to a Thai house for a meal but this time I was going to do it right! I carefully put on a simple cotton wrap-around skirt, white blouse with a set of Thai beads, and white sandals. Then confidently I set off.

I arrived at the large white house at the edge of the Dara Campus at six o'clock as directed. When the cook came to the door she seemed confused and as she did not understand English I, too, felt confused. There were children I knew playing in the yard, one of which was a Dara student, so I asked if her mother was expecting me. The answer was, "Oh, yes, but Mother has gone for a walk." What to do? Since I wasn't invited into the house, I watched the children play badminton for a while and then went over to the volleyball court where the Dara girl's team was practicing.

In a half hour or so, a Thai lady appeared and asked me if I was Acharn Jackie. She said she was Acharn Somsri's cousin, visiting from California, and had heard I was coming to dinner. She invited me into the house and we sat and visited for about fifteen minutes before Acharn Somsri returned. Again I saw I was wrongly dressed. Everyone wore jeans including our hostess, Acharn Somsri. Casual is the word for Thai entertainment.

After another half hour or so of visiting, we went into an eating area where there were about ten tempting dishes of Thai food on the table and a big pot of rice. Children ran in and out of the house while the three of us sat down to eat. Later the children stopped long enough to fill a plate and casually eat on chairs around the room.

It took a while for me to get used to this very informal entertaining but I liked it and was determined to try it when I returned to the states. I think, though, that I would make an effort to be at home when guests arrived! In Thailand although punctuality is not a priority, visiting with guests seems much more important than food and setting. How nice!

I admired Acharn Somsri, and she was very patient with me as I learned to adapt to a different and new method of teaching. Thais are very polite, never showing any displeasure with a foreigner, and while this is all very nice, you don't always know where you stand. Thais are restrained in their actions. I am exuberant with an abundance of energy. I tried to slow my pace all the while I was in their country and possibly succeeded at times, but I do know that they always treated me with respect and kindness in spite of my brash ways.

Since my fellow teachers seemed to have enjoyed the luncheon I served them in the fall, I decided before my second Christmas to try a party. By this time I had acquired some Thai furnishings— mats on the floor, several of the small Thai tables on which they serve food and floor pillows for comfort. My guest list included ten teachers and three children. A big crowd for my small one room apartment!

This time we sat on the floor and I served "Thai Spaghetti" which means I made the sauce "pet" or hot. In addition we had a molded salad with pineapple and cabbage, a tossed vegetable salad, deviled eggs, and French bread with garlic butter. Not too strange for Thai tastes, I hoped! I thought I had fixed an enormous amount of spaghetti but it soon disappeared and I stopped to make more. The jello was only moderately successful until someone thought of putting it on the garlic bread and then it became a big hit.

Since the teachers had shared and enjoyed the egg salad sandwich I had brought to school one day, the next thing I knew the deviled eggs were also perched atop French bread and quickly devoured. Naturally the next step was to make spaghetti sandwiches while we all doubled over in laughter. Thais do not normally eat bread, but probably because no one had ever served them French bread with garlic butter. Ten teachers rapidly finished off two long loaves.

Soon everyone was complaining about being "imm", stuffed, so I suggested we hold off on the ice cream sundaes until after I showed pictures. When they heard that I was serving ice cream with chocolate sauce and nuts—they quickly cleared the table, I mean the floor, and were ready for dessert. I filled bowls with huge portions of ice cream while others ladled on enormous helpings of nuts and chocolate sauce. They groaned the whole time they ate, but licked their bowls clean.

All collapsed on the floor while I set up the projector which was ready with two trays of slides. These included pictures of Dara, the teachers and a trip three teachers took with my son and me. Slides were not a part of their lives so they were excited to see themselves enlarged upon the wall. One small boy clapped with glee every time he saw his mother on the "TV"! During the pictures one husband arrived to pick up his wife and was quickly shooed away. He told us that he had anticipated this when he turned the corner by my house and heard us laughing almost half a block away! I felt a real kinship with this group of teachers and was much closer to having real Thai friends than I ever imagined. I decided this was the best Christmas party I'd ever had.

The following week Acharn Loar invited me to her home. Her husband was the Manager of the Thai Christian School in Chiang Mai and this turned out to be a pre-Christmas party for the school staff. I was not only the single outsider, but the one farang. Picture us out in the garden-patio-area, under a full moon which kept peeking through towering coconut palms. Four little barbecue pots were set along the paths and five or six people hovered over each cooking delicious pieces of marinated meat, while munching on the food they had taken from two long picnic tables. There were huge platters of cold meats spread on beds of greens, bowls of pork crackling, pots of delicious Thai soup, meat and vegetable dishes, baskets of fruits, platters of cucumber, cabbage, and onions.

Some people sat while most just walked around and reached for whatever they wanted. No serving spoons were used and you just helped yourself with chopsticks or your tablespoon. Whiskey, wine, and cold drinks were also served. Everyone in Thailand knew a little English and all were anxious to talk with a native speaker, but they were also very shy about it, so I appreciated the many who made an effort to spend time with me. This constant stream of people coming and going made me feel very much a part of the group.

After singing Christmas carols on that warm night, under the full moon and palm trees, we went into the house for a more formal type of program. They had set up a loud speaker since we were all sitting on the floor in two different rooms and couldn't see each other. The teacher who seemed to be in charge handed out a program song sheet which included some scripture, prayer and carols. Then came a talk by the manager, a beautiful gentle soul who was greatly respected by all the school staff. He presented a small gift to each of them and they took turns speaking with much laughter, joking, and teasing. Each one also greeted me before continuing with their talk. These were all vibrant young Thais whom I would like to know better and I felt it a rare privilege to be included in this gathering.

What a rich experience it was to share in the lives, homes, and families of those I met during my two year visit to Thailand. We laughed, we cried, we shared. Maybe I didn't make many "intimate" friends, but I did feel warmly accepted and included in their lives.

THE NIGHT
I DIDN'T SPEAK UP

I detest those times in life when an old memory crops up and reminds me of something in the past that I would much rather forget. Remembering it I again feel guilty and find myself going over and over the incident, thinking of how I might have done things differently. Several days later the memory fades away, but in the meantime I have been miserable.

This happened to me recently when I read the obituary of Dr. Albert Pickerell in the *San Francisco Chronicle*. Immediately I was back in Chiang Mai at a dinner party honoring Dr. and Mrs. Pickerell. The host was the governor of a nearby province and now I remembered his comments, my thoughts, and then my silence.

I had met Al Pickerell and his wife BJ at a party in Berkeley where he was a Professor specializing in media law at the University's School of Journalism. In 1954 Pickerell had received a Fulbright Scholarship to serve for one year as a lecturer at Thammasat

University in Bangkok. Besides being the first distinguished visiting professor he came to be greatly respected and loved by the Thai community for helping establish Thammasat's own School of Journalism. Now he was being asked to return and receive honors from both the University and his former students.

I received a letter from his wife, BJ, asking me to help make reservations and plan some local trips around Chiang Mai after their time in Bangkok. She remembered enjoying their visits there before and also the area's reputation for being cooler than the oppressive heat of Bangkok which they would want to escape after the ceremonies.

BJ specifically asked for reservations at the Railroad Hotel where they had regularly stayed on their trips north. Now the Railroad Hotel was not a place I would have chosen for visiting guests, being what we would probably call a one or two star establishment. It was located on the edge of town, across the street from the railroad station, and far from any of Chiang Mai's interesting sights. Most visitors wanted to stay in one of the more modern hotels in the center of town where they could walk to shops, see the Wats, and be near the exciting Night Market. But I made the reservation and eagerly awaited their arrival.

During the week before their scheduled visit to Chiang Mai, I was delighted and surprised to see many articles about them in the daily *Bangkok Post.* They were the "toast of the city" and each day there were stories and pictures of honors received and parties attended. I was impressed!

Friday was the big day and my plans were made. BJ was to phone me after they settled in at the Hotel, but when the call came she was very apologetic. Evidently all their plans had changed and they didn't really need my help. It seemed that the Governor of the adjoining province south of Chiang Mai had been one of Al's students at Thammasat University and had flown to Bangkok for the celebrations then insisted on taking over their visit to Chiang Mai. He would be in charge. BJ felt terrible but we both understood the Thai culture and wouldn't do anything to offend the Governor!

He had planned a small banquet for the Pickerells that night and BJ asked that I be included so I agreed to be at the Railroad Hotel at the appointed time to join them for dinner. At least I would see my friends for one evening.

After a quick hug, we were escorted to a big black ominous looking car with tinted windows, which with others like it, was parked in front of the hotel. I felt as though I were an intruder in this large party of Thai officials so I just sat back and watched and listened.

When we pulled up to the Poy Luang Hotel, I was delighted. This was one of my favorites. In fact, just a few weeks before I had been in charge of a large farewell dinner party here. Several members of the Mission community were returning to the States and I had planned a fun evening of good food and entertainment. The hotel management had been very accommodating and we had met many times to make arrangements.

Now I was the first to step out of this imposing automobile and the Thai staff, immediately recognizing me, greeted me enthusiastically with many bows and wais. They appeared thrilled to see Acharn Jackie and welcomed me as an honored guest. I quickly explained that I was not in charge but only the guest of the Governor who had already left the car to stand ignored and seemingly surprised at the fuss being made over me. As quickly as I could I quietly disappeared into the crowd.

Dinner was magnificent. I ate delicious Thai dishes that I had never seen or tasted in my eighteen months in Thailand. There were so many courses and varieties of food, that I was unable to keep count, but one I shall never forget was the large platter bearing a whole fish covered with a steaming black bean sauce. This was a rare delicacy only served on special occasions and had such a mellow taste, with the sauce so surprisingly mild and sweet, I just sat savoring it letting the conversation flow around me.

The Governor began to talk. He was saying something about the Tribal people and I put down my fork to listen. As he spoke my stomach turned and I was no longer hungry. He was bragging about how he had shown a group of them they were not welcome in his province. He proudly told how he had taught them a lesson so they would never return.

Among my friends in the Mission community, Paul and Elaine were two of my favorites. Intelligent and caring, they worked among the Tribal peoples and had done a myriad of things to improve their lives, from distributing malaria pills to creating their first written languages. Elaine also helped found the Chiang Mai Tribal Craft shop which specialized in handmade articles sewn by the women. In fact living conditions in whole villages had changed because of them.

Just the previous week Paul had told a group of us about a small community of Lisu who had settled south of Chiang Mai. These people moved often as they looked for new land for their crops, clearing as usual with slash and burn, the only way they knew.

This small group of Lisus had been awakened in the middle of the night by several large open trucks roaring into their little compound. As the people crawled out of the shelters, they were roughly rounded up and herded into the back of trucks by men dressed in typical khaki police uniforms. No one was allowed to retrieve any belongings—additional warm clothing, simple cooking utensils, their small supply of rice, blankets, or hidden money.

A week later they were found starving and cold in an isolated area of the northern rain forest to which they had been taken and dropped. Paul told us of how he had arranged for other groups to take them in and share their own meager supplies until the Lisu folk were able to move on and take care of themselves.

And here as I sat at dinner listening to the Governor I discovered who had been responsible for relocating those impoverished people. I thought of the contrast of how this Thai official treated those who had lived in his country for centuries, in comparison to a couple from Oregon who saw them with love and compassion and whose aim was to help and be supportive.

I wanted to tell this to the Governor, explain how destructive and cruel his efforts were and ask why he didn't join forces with the many volunteers who were eager to educate these folk to a better way of life. But I was his guest. It would embarrass the Pickerells. It might even be counter-productive for Paul and Elaine if they were found to be involved, as had happened many times with volunteers who opposed the methods of Thai officials.

I kept my mouth shut. I didn't respond. I didn't tell him what I thought. This was the night I didn't speak up and it continues to haunt me to this day.

A BROTHER'S ADVICE
UNHEEDED

Whrit my brother, Pete, had heard I was going to live in the Golden Triangle of northern Thailand for two years, he couldn't believe it. "That place is too dangerous!" he admonished. "Don't go! Everyone knows it's the drug capital of the world." But I ignored his warning, knowing I was quite capable of taking care of myself—and for months I had proven his fears groundless having nothing but positive and wonderful experiences.

Then one quiet Sunday evening about 8:40 p.m., as I was wrapping a gift at the table on my second story screened-in porch, I thought the world had come to an end. This was a very **real** feeling, one I could never have imagined.

A loud explosion suddenly pierced my eardrums and sucked the breath from my lungs. My body felt as though it had been punched and I swayed on my feet, grabbing the table for support. Through the screens I saw palm branches madly thrashing and beyond brilliant yellow and blue flashes lit up the sky. It went on and on. It may have been only seconds but I felt I was living in slow motion as the whipping branches and flashing lights continued. My terror was astounding. I couldn't breathe.

Surrounded by loud crashes and noises I could not fathom what was happening. I stood transfixed. Was I about to die? Gradually my mind cleared. I was alive, breathing and whole. The noises were abating. Silence. The trees swayed gently. No more flashing lights.

I lived in a quiet neighborhood of homes behind some schools several miles from the center of Chiang Mai. What could explode so close with such force? There were no factories or gas stations in the area, only simple wooden homes, a church, a temple, and a few small shops. Yet an explosion of some kind had taken place. A BIG ONE!

I needed to know what had happened. The whole area was now completely dark. I turned to feel my way through my living room to the back porch where I could hear my neighbors were gathering. I was barefoot! We never wore shoes in our Thai houses so we could protect our beautifully polished teak floors. Now my tentatively shuffling feet could feel disaster. Broken plaster, dishes, pictures, and furniture were everywhere, and reaching for a flashlight in a kitchen drawer as I passed, I tiptoed very cautiously through the debris to where my thongs waited outside my back door.

All was confusion as neighbors from the four apartments assembled. My first action was to stop Donna who seemed dazed and walked barefoot toward me oblivious of the broken pottery, plants, dirt, and baskets in her path. I helped her to sit down on the steps and brushed the trash off the soles of her feet while someone retrieved her slippers. She gradually calmed down. Everyone began talking and asking questions. Suddenly we noticed a bright glow in the sky just beyond our property and realized it was a house engulfed in flames. With many friends living nearby, our concern mounted.

Noises increased as people and cars poured into the area. I heard sounds of approaching sirens. Carefully we made our way down the stairs and headed toward the side road. Across the field dust and smoke were rising behind the International School and towering flames roared from the Filbeck's home. We had been with this family only a few hours earlier at the Community Church Vesper Service and now frantically wondered where they were. I wanted to do something to help but everything seemed hopelessly confused.

Our small group, holding hands for support, both emotional and physical, approached the destruction, but there was nothing to be done, the house would soon be completely destroyed. Then we noticed that the ten-foot brick and stone wall surrounding General Li's house was down leaving an enormous crater. Beyond, what had been a massive three-story house, was now only reinforced concrete pillars and lonely walls. Just a shell surrounded by rubble.

In a state of shock and disbelief we saw that the Chiang Mai International School just behind the General's house had also been badly damaged. It was all too much. Part of the second floor at the closest end of the building perilously hung over the courtyard and I realized it was where my classroom had been last year.

I taught fourth grade at this school and my room had looked out over the high wall into General Li's compound below. I had heard stories of how he had been a General in the Kuomintang Army in China and when the Communists overran the country he and many other military leaders fled south. As a side to their military responsibilities, it was well known that these men also dealt in jade and opium, and as the KMT leaders fled to Taiwan, these traitors ran to remote areas in Burma, Thailand, and Laos.

After arriving in Thailand, they convinced the government that in return for being allowed to remain and become citizens they would stop their illegal trading and cooperate with the Thai army to help rid this northern area of communist activity. They stayed but everyone knew that the trading did not cease. They were still in the drug business with no fear of being expelled. In Thailand government corruption is a way of life and surely many palms had been crossed with silver.

I remembered sitting at my desk the previous year with my

thirteen international students, wondering what I would do if I ever heard gunfire from the walled compound next door. This high structure with broken bottles and barbed wire cemented along the top was a sinister sight and the only plan I could come up with, was to have my students fall to the floor and crawl to the back of the room. They certainly could not go outside on the exposed porch at the side of our building. But I wasn't really very concerned because these things never happen to us, do they? Now I could only think how lucky it was that this explosion had occurred on a Sunday evening when school wasn't in session and I thanked God for that small blessing in all this mayhem.

By now it was clear to me that all this had not been an accident. Some kind of bomb must have been planted with the intention of blowing up the opium warlord's home. At this time we had no idea as to the number of deaths in this destruction, but it was later reported in the local newspapers that only one person had been killed, a gentleman who lived next door to the Filbecks. However, a reliable friend in the international community said he saw a truck pull up to the front of the demolished house immediately after the explosion and watched as a large number of bodies were thrown into the back and hurriedly driven away. We guessed that the government was playing it safe by not disclosing the deaths of these Chinese drug dealers, but all this we would learn later. We would also learn that General Li had been in Bangkok on the fateful evening visiting his daughter. Police later identified the bomber as "Noom," a right-hand man of Khun Sa, the other major opium warlord of the Golden Triangle. He was never found.

For now we were relieved to learn that the Filbecks were safe. They had returned home from church an hour before the explosion and had taken their Thai servants to town for dinner and shopping. David Filbeck told us later, "I left home at 8 p.m. to go to the Night Market. About 8:45 I heard the explosion but paid no attention, so imagine our shock when we arrived home at ten to find our rented house burned to the ground and everything destroyed. It's certainly the most terrible thing that has happened to us since living in Chiang Mai," he lamented.

We tried to console the family, then weary and shaken returned to our apartment building. The yard swarmed with Thai and international friends checking to see if we were safe and they returned to our rooms with us. For the first time we really saw the enormity of the damage.

Donna found her kitchen cupboards hanging perilously off her walls and all dishes and supplies in a broken heap on the floor. My plastered living room ceiling had now settled in the middle of the room beneath the dust from the attic which was still descending on my furniture. A new set of hand painted celedon dishes must have left the shelf, become airborne, and then broken into a thousand fragments as they landed. All my shelves were empty, and vases, books, and ornaments piled in unrecognizable heaps around the room so that I felt an almost hysterical joy when I found any precious item intact. Finding my bed completely covered with dust, dirt, and plaster, I wondered when I would ever be able to sleep in it again!

Recovering from bomb blast!

Wearily I returned to the porch where I had been working before the explosion and found my neighbors looking through wooden studs from their room into mine. The wall separating our apartments was no longer there, so we began to laugh helplessly and joked about having a slumber party. Later I was horrified when I found a large, framed picture from that adjoining wall on the floor on the opposite side of my room and realized that it must have missed my head by inches as it flew past me. Strange how I had been completely unaware of things flying through the air and walls tumbling down at the time of the explosion.

Friends quickly decided to take us to their homes for the night. Returning to Ruth's, although I had already been assured of plenty of help, I was relieved to escape from the reminders of the overwhelming cleanup ahead of me.

Later, trying to fall asleep, I could not stop thinking of my brother's words. He had warned me of danger and it had come. It was the most terrifying experience of my life. I could still see the thrashing trees and flaring lights which I now knew to be power transformers in the neighborhood blowing up from the force of the explosion. My fear had been brief but overwhelming. When my brother heard about it he would say I was wrong to have come to this place, but as my eyelids became heavy and sleep forced itself upon me, I realized that there was risk everywhere in the world. No one could completely escape it and I knew I would never give up the challenge of new adventures to hide at home.

VISITOR FROM HOME

There I was, once again, at the Don Muan Airport in Bangkok looking for someone through the custom's window, but this time I was on the outside looking in. Daughter Lorie, my first visitor from home, would soon be coming down the ramp from her plane and I had been standing there for over an hour remembering my arrival a year before. No one had been there to meet me and I did **not** want that to happen to my daughter on her first overseas trip. Her Mom was going to be the very first thing she saw when she looked through that glass.

I had hardly slept all night for excitement and yet there was also a smidgen of anxiety. Lorie and I generally had a very good mother/daughter relationship, but we had also had some tense moments in recent years, especially when we had been together for extended periods of time. How would it be now for three weeks?

I knew that Lorie was under a lot of pressure at the University, working on her PhD, doing research, writing a dissertation and also being a TA which meant preparing regular lectures. Once here would she be able to leave all that behind and relax? I was rested, eager, and full of energy but I told myself, I must slow down—and definitely not be too "motherly".

There was also the question of her father's death four years earlier. My time here in Thailand had given me a chance to think about it and come to terms but what did Lorie think? We had never discussed it. She and Lee were not close—had never really understood each other. How often I'd had to smooth things over between them. Lorie, so private, never discussisng her feelings, even with me. She would leave Lee feeling terribly hurt if they went on errands in the car and she didn't talk. He'd be offended and was never able to accept her silences. Did she feel any guilt because of their poor relationship? Any regrets? How had she handled his death. It should be discussed sometime but would she resent my bringing it up?

I looked at my watch. Where was she? My eyes were weary of peering through that large plate glass window that separated travelers from anxious friends and family. Then, "Ah!" It was like a universal sigh. Figures had begun to trickle down the ramp from the plane and into the building. My heart skipped a beat. Was that her? That attractive, young woman striding through the crowd looking for her luggage with the air of a seasoned traveler. Was that stunning, smartly dressed woman the same child who had run about wearing torn jeans in her elementary and high school years. My camera was ready and I captured her arrival in the lens.

"Here I am, Mom. I made it!" We were hugging. "You didn't tell me the plane stopped in Taipei! We all had to get off, leaving our luggage and spend the night there—and me with no carry-on!"

"Oh, Lorie. I didn't know. I'm so sorry!"

"No problem. I got to see a little of another country and I bought a Chinese toothbrush."

Her hugs and smiles told me I was forgiven. "Come on, let's get a taxi." I took her arm and as we walked I explained how airport cabbies in Bangkok were notorious for bilking unsuspecting tourists, and then I impressed her by negotiating with three different drivers before we choose one.

"You speak Thai so well!" Lorie exclaimed as we headed into town. I didn't disillusion her with the knowledge that my Thai was mostly limited to directions, greetings, and ordering food.

We were staying at the Bangkok Christian Guest house which was sponsored by the Church of Christ of Thailand, the umbrella organization for the many missionary groups in the country. It was like a home away from home with simple, cozy rooms and the most interesting travelers to talk to: workers from the UN, Peace Corps personnel, and a host of folk coming out of Cambodia, Burma, Vietnam, etc. on diplomatic and humanitarian missions. We all ate together in a family style dining room where every meal companion had an interesting story to tell.

"This is really great, Mom," Lorie whispered, flushed with excitement. I relaxed. If only it could last for the next three weeks.

We did the tourist things in Bangkok before heading for Chiang Mai. Lorie especially enjoyed meeting the deaf and dumb artists who sold their pictures in the Pot Porn (red light) District. These young men were great fun and I had a wonderful time watching Lorie deal with them through sign language, finger pointing, and smiles. Their colorful paintings depicted scenes from all over Thailand, and we had a terribly difficult time choosing which to buy. The result was that our homes back in California eventually had many walls decorated with Thai artwork.

A visit to the ancient city of Ayuthaya is a must for any visitor to Thailand, so of course we went. Lorie, fascinated by everything, looked out of the bus windows during the two hour bus ride. "Look at those villages! Do they really sleep in those open houses? It's all so green—are those rice fields? How beautiful! I love the quiet here in the country after Bangkok."

And later as we strolled through the overgrown ruins of what had once been a city bigger than either Paris or London in their heyday, we tried to imagine it as it was. Tried to see again the temples and palaces linked by canals and all built on a manmade island. A place of such glittering opulence which, though it astonished foreign visitors, incited the Burmese to savagely tear it apart in search of booty.

"How could they!" Lorie sighed.

We stood in the shadow of large headless Buddhas which loomed silently, looked at the three central chedis that had been restored and the many magnificent wats that had also been rebuilt around the perimeter but it was the ruins of the old city which intrigued us.

After several hours of walking in the tropical sun, we were ready for our luxurious return trip to Bangkok aboard the Oriental Queen, a boat run by the Oriental Hotel. The river breeze coupled with a deluxe buffet lunch soon revived our energy and we hung over the rail shooting pictures of the many unusual boats and barges, picturesque farmlands, and quaint villages along the shore, and then finally the buildings of industry as we approached Bangkok.

Lorie and I had been together constantly for three days. I had made an effort to give her space when I could—like strolling around the boat by myself—however, after dinner one night I heard the half expected announcement, "I'm going out for coffee. Saw a little coffee shop down the street. Don't wait up." And she was gone.

I knew she could only take so much "togetherness" and I accepted that but it was hard not to worry about her out there alone in a strange city. I didn't let her know I was still awake when she returned.

The next day after a visiting two plantations, one sugar and the other coconut, we stopped at the floating market for a glimpse of the still-active water-borne life of Thailand. At one time Bangkok had been the Venice of Asia, full of canals and rivers, but now most of them were filled in for roads and freeways. However, the floating market did remain and was still a wonderful sight. As we stepped down to the river we saw hundreds of boats, loaded with fruits, vegetables, dried fish, rice, and a myriad of other locally produced foods. Each craft was paddled by a woman wearing a broad-brimmed lamp shade hat and a ready smile for the many clicking cameras.

Most tourists stopped on the dock to watch but Lorie quickly exclaimed, "Let's hire a boat and go for a ride!" Before I knew it there she was negotiating through hand signals and smiles with a lady willing to take us.

Within a few minutes we were seated in one of the wide flat-bottomed boats, paddled through the middle of the market. Vendors swung close to offer us fried bananas, fresh coconut milk, and custard-like sweets wrapped in banana leaves, but we carefully chose only a few bananas not wanting to risk upset tummies on this trip.

And next came the snake farm. I had hoped to avoid this as I'd been once before and once was enough for me! But Lorie insisted. "Oh, Mom, snakes won't hurt you!" So there we were sitting under a huge, shady monkeypod tree while on a platform in front of us young men displayed a variety of king cobras, Russell vipers, and banded kraits. Soon both of us had cases of gooseflesh and I couldn't have been more relieved when I heard the sweet words, "Mom, let's get out of here!" As I stood up to leave a writhing snake thumped onto my chair—a well planned move by one of the young men which I did not appreciate.

Lunch and a show at the Rose Garden gave Lorie a real taste of Thailand's many colorful traditions. We saw the fingernail dance, sword fighting, Thai foot boxing, a tribal dance, cock fighting, and a bamboo dance. Then after watching elephants perform outside the theater Lorie clambered up on one for her first elephant ride. "Take a picture, Mom. Wait til my students see this!"

Next day was Kanchanaburi and the Bridge on the River Kwai, made famous by the book written by Pierre Boulle, later made into a Hollywood film.

In a van traveling to the town 122 km northwest of Bangkok, we met a gentleman from England who had once been a prisoner of war here. He had slaved for the Japanese on the notorious railroad where an estimated 100,000 oppressed laborers and 16,000 Allied prisoners of war had died from beatings, starvation, disease, and exhaustion. He expressed his resentment at the glory allocated to those who worked on the bridge, as depicted in the movie, while his job of helping build tracks along the steep cliffs and through the jungles had been much more difficult. He told us how the British prisoners had tried their utmost to do the worst job possible often using rotting wood supports. Then he talked of his desire to return to this historic, disastrous place but also admitted the anxiety he felt doing it. It was a difficult journey for the old gentleman but I supposed he needed to bring closure to his experience. Meeting him certainly made our journey more meaningful.

"I can't believe the people I am meeting," Lorie said, as we left the van, having reached Kanchanaburi. "Every day there's someone with an unusual story. I don't meet these kind of people in a year and you are surrounded by them. How do you handle it?"

I reminded her that in my letters home I had written how overwhelmed I had felt by all the new experiences I was having.

As we walked past the endless rows of war graves marking the resting places of all those Allied soldiers we didn't have much to say to each other. Our thoughts were with the tragedy of those who had suffered and died there.

I wondered how the old English gentleman was doing.

After our visit to the bridge, we boarded a train in Kanchanaburi and continued to travel west toward the town of Nam Tok, the termination station for the Thailand-Burma railroad built by the prisoners. The train ride was terrifying as the tracks hung precariously on the side of the cliffs and Lorie sat on the steps of the coach car looking down several hundred feet into the river below. I bit my tongue knowing that any overly concerned "Mother" comments would not be welcomed! We traveled at a snail's pace stopping often for the engineers to get out and inspect the track in front of us to be sure it was safe. Not the most assuring activity for passengers! It was difficult to imagine how these tracks had been laid in such steep terrain and we heaved a huge sigh of relief when we arrived in Nam Tok where we planned a short stay.

This remote area on the Meklang River, also known as the Kwai Yai, is beautiful with waterfalls, caves, and pristine jungle. We spent our time riding long boats up and down the river, observing the people and industry. Many villagers cut bamboo from the jungles, sliding their harvest to the edge of the river and then making bamboo rafts for floating the product to market. In simple shelters added to the tops of the rafts, the families cooked their meals, and fished as the traveled.

When we saw the Raft Hotel on the shore of the river, we were ready to hop off our long boat and sign up for a room. What a perfect place, so quiet, calming, and peaceful. We saw floating bamboo huts with double or single beds, modest toilet facilities, a bar, "stage," pet monkeys and a crocodile. We stopped to pet the monkey and enjoy a cool drink at the bar. As I dutifully took pictures of Lorie with her new monkey friends, an elephant came silently out of the jungle behind us, stopped for a drink, looked us over and retreated. Lorie raced to the edge of the dock. "Quick, Mom. No one will believe this is me with a real wild elephant!"

Our destination was the River Kwai Village and our stay was enhanced by the fact that there were few other guests in evidence and the young men attendants thought Lorie was *su-i* (beautiful!) and were also impressed that an *Acharn* was staying there. We received the royal treatment. We had lots of fun communicating, they in their broken English and we with our limited Thai. They flocked around us at all meals and hovered over us as we played cards in the lounge. That evening ended with our being serenaded by the head waiter with his guitar and another with a mouth organ. They sang both Thai and American songs, ending with "I Love Chiang Mai," as they knew that was where we would soon be headed. After a number of songs, I quietly left the room and headed for bed. This was another chance for Lorie to have some time on her own to privately make her own Thai friends.

The only drawback was that Lorie was awakened when something plopped on her bed in the middle of the night— cockroaches! I awoke to find her crouching on top of the toilet calling out to me, "Kill them, Mom! Kill them all!" I assured her that if we left the lights and air conditioning on all night they would go away. Eventually I coaxed her back to bed and I went to sleep wearing a smile. It took some doing but sometimes it was OK to be a "mother."

FALLING IN LOVE WITH THAILAND

After our train trip north to Chiang Mai, Lorie relaxed for a few days and enjoyed getting acquainted with my Thai city and Thai home. "Gorgeous," she had enthused at first sight of my tree house. I could see she had already fallen in love with Thailand, but I knew the best was yet to come. For the time being, however, here was a chance for her to safely take off on her own and explore a unique foreign city with no trouble in finding her way home.

After her first evening in the Night Market she exclaimed, "It's just like a US fair or flea market." At every booth we passed Lorie was tempted by the plethora of lovely Thai crafts and I cautioned her to slow down—she had another 10 days to explore this unusual area. Friends took us to the McKean Leprosy Center and she was as amazed as I had been when I first heard the story of how much had been done to rehabilitate those unfortunate people.

Lorie's first July 4th in a foreign country presented her with a chance to attend the American Consulate party in Chiang Mai and meet some of my friends there. The day was a scorcher but we headed off in the late afternoon looking forward to some good American food! When she saw the array of food and drinks being passed her first question was, "Are missionary children allowed to drink beer?" I laughed, appreciating her sensitivity to my position, and encouraged her to enjoy herself!

Within a few minutes after arriving, I saw a tall young man coming in our direction. It was Connie whom I had met during my first visit to the Consulate. At that time he and Tom had just been assigned to Chiang Mai to head up the USDEA (United States Drug Enforcement Agency) in the Golden Triangle area. Both were single as no married couples had been allowed to occupy this position since the wife and child of a USDEA director had been kidnapped and murdered a few years before.

At that first meeting Connie, Tom, and I were soon deep in conversation about who we were, where we had come from, and why we were in Chiang Mai, but I never saw two men disappear so fast as when I told them I was working for my church! Later, at a Christmas party, I also experienced their displeasure with missionaries when I heard them loudly and pointedly, criticizing the church, well aware that I could hear them.

But now I had a stunning daughter at my side. Graciously I introduced Connie to Lorie—my daughter who was getting her PhD in Criminology from the University of California! He perked up immediately and as I was soon ignored, I left to talk to other friends. When Lorie joined me later she had two comments to make.

"Mom, Connie told me he felt badly about the way he scoffed at you when you two first met. (It would have been nice if he had had the courage to tell me!) AND—he wanted my phone number so he could take me out to dinner. Can you see me, a bleeding-heart liberal sustaining a conversation with a conservative like him!" Obviously the phone number had not been passed on.

We enjoyed the traditional U.S. 4th of July display of fireworks out over the Ping River. As they had run out of hot dogs and hamburgers at the Consulate we headed for the night market to finish dinner and sat in a cool spot at an outdoor restaurant down by the river. I ordered a small tray of cold cuts but when I asked, in my limited Thai, for some rolls, the waiter brought us spoons, forks and napkins. Not exactly what we wanted but our laughs were worth it.

The next night we were invited to Donna's for dinner with friends from the States. After the meal Lorie returned to our room to get a piece of the bronze ware she had purchased in Bangkok. Unfortunately, as she picked up one of the knives and pulled it from the plastic bag, it badly sliced her left, middle index finger. Hurriedly she returned to Donna's with her hand wrapped in a towel, blood flowing freely.

Luckily one of the guests, a public health nurse, quickly took over, held the finger under cold water and then iced it. The gash looked deep so we rushed over to check with Dr. Guyer, head of our Presbyterian Hospital nearby, who said stitches were in order.

Lorie was skeptical of Thai hospitals, but said she was reassured when she saw this one had electricity! A female doctor with two attendants made her lie down and gave her a shot of novocain. When the stitches started, Lorie gave me a look of reproach. "Mom, where is your camera? Did I do all this for nothing?"

A few days later on a four hour bus trip north to Chiang Rai, I wondered if this were the time for a serious talk. Lorie seemed much more relaxed than when she had first arrived. I offered some leading questions like, "How are you doing? Any problems dealing with Dad's death?" etc. Her answers were just like Lee's. "Everything's fine. No problem." I shuddered as I recalled hearing these same words from him, years before.

And then there had been those devestating written
words . . .
 I didn't know whether to be elated or terrified when the
news came that Lee's Dad was in the hospital with pneumonia.
This was it. We had attended a Jungian Conference at Asilomar

in Monterey a few years before, and during a consultation with the leader about Lee's condition, he told me that when Lee's Dad died, it could either release Lee or take him. Now, which would it be?

Lee quickly boarded a train for Santa Barbara and was able to spend one day at his father's bedside before he died. As soon as I finished teaching that day I was in my car on my way to join the family.

Since Lee was the oldest son, his Mother asked him to give the eulogy at the Memorial service to be held the following Sunday. So Lee borrowed a typewriter from his brother and holed up in our motel room to write. I spent the time with his mother with whom I had been good friends from the start and it was easy to sit with her and talk about her life with Dad. The two of them had traveled all over the world together, so I concentrated on these excursions, rather than their time as a family.

When I returned to our motel room that night, Lee was eager to share what he had written. So I sat on the edge of the bed and read. I was shocked. I could not believe what I was reading. He had made his dad a saint!

What to do? Lee had worked on this all day. He was drained. He was exhausted. How could I tell him that this was not what he really thought of his Father. I also worried about what it would do to him when he realized what he had done.

I sat quietly for a few moments while he waited for my approval. I needed an answer to my prayer of desperation— FAST! It came. I knew that several of his aunts, his father's sisters, were coming to the service. Over the years I had heard hilarious stories about their childhood on the prairies where their father was an itinerant preacher. The stories about the missionary barrels they received with the buttons cut off all the dresses and shirts. About how their father had had to bury meat at night in the back field because that was how he was often paid and they couldn't eat it all. And, he hadn't written about his mother and her part in dad's life.

Very gently I suggested that he had left out the humor and fun things that had happened to this family and that maybe the sisters would be hurt if they weren't included. And certainly he might want to mention his mother in the eulogy.

He looked pained. He put his head in his hands. He said he couldn't do it. It was too much. I reminded him that he had one more day to work on this. "Let's get some sleep and I'll help you in the morning." Reluctantly he agreed.

The eulogy was rewritten and a more human man appeared. Lee seemed relieved. Following the service and after taking care of arrangements for his mother, we headed home back up highway 101. Lee drove. I sat and pondered. He wouldn't talk. I tried to convince myself that things would get better. But my heart floundered. Even the slightest sense of relief remained elusive.

Two weeks later Lee took his life.

Lorie is so much like the father she never really knew. Both scholars who liked to research and write. Both politically liberal, concerned about the plight of man, the world, and the pain people suffered. Both people who did **not** like to disclose feelings! I sighed and gave up for the time being.

Lorie oohed and ahhed over the luscious, green rice fields, the plodding water buffalo pulling plows, workers in straw hats knee deep in water planting rice. After a while she looked around at our fellow passengers and informed me, "Look, a Buddhist monk. Now we'll have a safe trip." I knew she had heard about the alarming number of bus accidents in Thailand as drivers drove too fast on the windy, narrow, hilly roads, and we had already seen buses that had crashed and been abandoned. I was glad we need no longer worry about ours!

Being a criminology student, she was especially alert when the bus was stopped several times during our four-hour trip and police officers strode menacingly up and down the aisles. They peered into faces, felt some of the bags, and asked to see various identifications. One officer stopped next to Lorie and asked in

English what country she was from. No one was detained. We wondered if the fact that we were Americans caused them to be more careful. I had been told that the police were very corrupt and that many of the Tribal people were forced to pay bribes in lieu of going to jail and were sometimes robbed under threat of arrest for no good reason.

Arriving in Chiang Rai we were picked up by my friends Elaine and Paul. They had just published the most documented book on the tribal people they worked with, called *Peoples of the Golden Triangle*. During my first year in Thailand I had traveled with Paul and Elaine to remote areas here in the north and I knew that Lorie would be as amazed as I was by the work they were doing.

Sure enough she was soon off with Paul to visit a school for Tribal children where he needed to take pictures for potential sponsors. A few hours later Lorie was back enthusiastically reporting the morning's activities. "It was amazing, those beautiful little children, all brought by their parents to have their pictures taken." Lorie was so excited about her visit, that though she sat at the lunch table with her favorite Thai dishes, she didn't put a bite of food in her mouth.

We listened with amused interest as she continued to talk non-stop. Those parents are so poor. They really need sponsors to help them. "Paul was so kind and gentle with the children, you should have seen him. I'm sure his pictures will bring in a ton of sponsors. I saw him speak gently to each set of parents and later he explained how he was encouraging them to learn Thai and see that their children learned it, too. He said they would never get citizenship papers without it."

In the afternoon they were off again, this time to take pictures at a hostel where older tribal children lived while attending school. Returning from this trip Lorie hurried into the room exclaiming, "Mom, I'm going to adopt a student! Paul says it's much harder to find sponsors for these older kids as most people want one of the cute little wide-eyed ones." What a joy for me to see this enthusiasm coming from the girl who had arrived from California just over a week before—quite weary from the pressures of graduate school.

She couldn't stop talking! "All I have to do is send a small check each month and it'll keep a student in school. Paul will pick one out for me and send me his name. I'm so excited!" I had hoped Lorie would enjoy this time with Paul and Elaine and it was turning out even better than I could ever have anticipated.

While riding with Paul, Lorie was getting a real education about their work and as we prepared for bed in their guest room that night, she expressed her appreciation of their philosophy. "I like it that they offer development aid, but they also make a big effort to encourage the people to maintain their own culture. They don't want them to look and act like us but it's an awfully difficult balance to maintain." While she laid out her clothes for our long trip in the morning, she continued, "Many of the young people get to see occasional American TV shows—then want to look and act like our kids. How sad."

Being a young woman with social concerns and honoring people's rights to make their own choices, Lorie expressed pleasure that Paul and Elaine didn't push family planning, but did provide information regarding alternative methods. I struggled to keep awake and listen to her reflections but as I drifted off to sleep the last thing I heard her say was, "I never knew missionaries did **this** kind of work. I like it."

The ride back to Chiang Mai was memorable. Elaine, always anxious to visit as many villages as possible so she could help the tribal woman develop their many skills for marketing in her cooperative Hill Tribe Craft shop in Chiang Mai, made several stops and Lorie was amazed and shocked by the primitive conditions she saw. "Oh my gosh, Mom. They don't have anything," she exclaimed. And it was true that most of those people lived on the very edge of survival.

While Paul and Elaine were busy, Lorie and I strolled along dusty roads observing village life. Of special interest were some huge ornamental gates in several of the villages usually located on a path at the upper ends of the village. We were warned that these magnificent structures were sacred and must not be defiled. Therefore, it was suggested, we should not even attempt to walk through one, but take the path around the side. The purpose of the gate and the wooden figures was to keep out evil spirits and protect the villagers from hawks and wildcats, leopards and tigers, illness and plague, leprosy and epilepsy, and other bad things. Each year they were rebuilt with two large posts and a crossbar, to which were added a variety of decorations made out of bamboo; leaves and carvings of wooden guns, crossbows, birds, and taboo signs to prevent evil spirits from entering. There was always at least one male and one female figure and while these figures seemed to exhibit sexual postures, we were told they were there only to indicate that this place belonged to human beings and evil spirits should stay in the forest!

Most amazing of all was the Spirit Swing built precariously at the edge of a level area. It consisted of a number of fragile looking poles tied together in a tent-like structure, from the middle of which a swing constructed of twines woven together hung down with a simple board to be used as a seat near ground level. It gave us shivers to envision anyone sitting on this frail, decrepit board and swinging out over the side of the hill. We understood this was used by the leaders of the village on New Year's Day, but women and children were also seen swinging wildly out into space. Since I am even afraid of a well built roller coaster, I couldn't imagine attempting to swing on the Spirit Swing—the village spirits would never be appeased by me!

We noticed women coming in from the forest with baskets filled with branches and twigs for cooking the evening meal. They looked old and tired and we assumed they were elderly, but many that we would have guessed to be in their 50's and 60's were actually in their late twenties or thirties. It was a hard life scratching out a living on the side of those hills. Undernourished children, some with rickets, wandered around listlessly chasing the chickens.

We watched women using many different types of frames for weaving, some built outside huts where the land had been cleared and raked. The women stood by them all day long, weaving colorful yards of material with intricate patterns and during the rainy season the frames are simply taken apart and stored. Other weavers sat on the floors of their verandas, using their hands and feet to control the frame.

Lorie and I were surprised to see a number of women wearing rows of silver bracelets. Back in the car on the ride to Chiang Mai, Elaine explained that these bracelets were their bank account! When they earned money from their weaving, they invested it in silver bracelets, which they wore until they needed cash. (A few months later Elaine called and asked me if I wanted to buy two large silver bracelets as a Karen tribal lady needed to pay for surgery.)

As a fourth grade school teacher in California, my class had learned about the mortar and pestle, used by California Indians to crush acorns for their meals. Here we saw the same method used by the tribal people, but in a more intricate manner. They used a large log which was controlled by a foot pedal to raise and lower the large pestle tied at the end. Rice was poured into a hollowed-out rock and a large amount could be crushed at one time. Often young girls, working in pairs, were responsible for this chore, one doing the crushing while the other tossed the grain into the air from a basket to rid the rice of the chaff.

Finally as we stepped over chickens, avoided scraggly looking dogs, and dodged the many little pigs scurrying around the village, we observed the various round trays and flat platforms where food was being dried. We were only able to identify chili peppers and sesame seeds and stayed clear of the trays that looked like dried crickets!

During the trip, we picked up additional passengers who needed transportation "down the road" or "to the next village." Paul always checked to see if they had their papers before he would offer a ride and we understood why when, as we headed south, we were stopped at a road block by six policemen who asked Paul to get out of the car and proceeded to talk to him for some time. Next they checked all our passenger's papers and our passports. Later Paul told us that the extent of this inquiry was unusual. But, you soon learned not to be surprised by anything, when traveling in the Golden Triangle.

Wherever we went, most of the village turned out to greet us and as there was always an abundance of children. Lorie and I wondered about their schooling. It seemed that as school was rather casual, whenever someone came to the village, it was a good opportunity to leave the "classroom." The school building itself was usually just a wooden platform with benches, possibly a counter for writing, a limited number of notebooks and hopefully a blackboard. There was no regular schedule for classes in these remote villages, but children are called together when someone with at least a 4th grade education came to the village and volunteered to teach them for a period of time.

It was the middle of the afternoon. "We're almost there!" Elaine shouted over the noise of the engine. "Now remember, no foreigners have ever been to this village before." She had heard about these rather desperate people and hoped she might be able to offer them some advice about their crafts which she would then proceed to sell for them. Paul, ever the obliging husband, turned off the main highway. Soon we bumped down a slightly level large path carved out of the side of the hill, a road obviously made by villagers, not by any machines. I was glad to be sitting in the back seat nearest the upside of the hill for Elaine was looking down a sharp bank into a creek far below. Lorie sat bravely in front with Paul and was careful not to describe to her fearful mother what was ahead of us. At one point Paul stopped the car and got out to inspect the road in front of us which suddenly dropped sharply down two to three feet before continuing across a shallow creek. At this point I told Paul I needed to stretch my legs so I gingerly climbed out of the car, hopped down the sharp drop, forded the creek, and waited for Paul a ways up the road. He had become an expert at driving in these conditions and soon maneuvered the car down the bank, across the stream and picked me up on the other side. As we continued, hopefully with the worst spots behind us, Paul commented that this was the poorest road he had been on in 26 years of travel in Asia.

After a brief visit with the leaders of the village we were invited into one of the homes where we all sat on the ground. Paul and Elaine continued to talk while Lorie and I looked on in amazement at these interesting people, their beautiful jewelry, unusual hats (Lorie has a collection!), and art objects. We were careful not to ask them to sell anything to us—not polite—so we sat quietly. The tribal people in their turn seemed intrigued by Lorie. She is a tall young lady, standing 5 foot 10 inches in her bare feet, but her platform sandals added another two inches to bring her up to 6 feet! With her long curly blonde hair, colorful floral blouse, and red slacks, she did stand out among these friendly people whose height averaged about 5 feet. Soon one of the ladies came forward with a woven conical hat and seemed to present it to Lorie in a questioning fashion. Elaine explained that she wondered if Lorie would like to buy it. It was a virgin's hat to be worn only before marriage and Lorie beamed as it was placed on her head. As I grabbed the camera out of my bag, she asked if there were people behind her for the picture—she wanted this to be special. When I told her they had just removed the side wall of the house so all the villagers could watch us, the smile increased and Lorie had the picture of a lifetime. When we left, our hands were full of unusual baskets, hats, and articles of clothing. We paid the asking price and everyone was happy—villagers and farangs alike.

Lorie with Thai treasures

I sat in the back of the car, surrounded by our purchases, tired and happy. Paul somehow gunned the motor and the car made it back across the stream, up the steep bank—down the narrow road. We were soon back on the smooth highway. Lorie sat dreamily in the front seat next to Paul as he drove us safely back to Chiang Mai. This had been another rare day and we will always be grateful to Paul and Elaine for sharing their lives and work so graciously with us,

The following week Lorie visited more tribal villages with my friends while I taught school. She also loved being on her own to go down town shopping and exploring. On the weekend we arrived at the bus station early in the morning and then sat in a crowded van for a four-hour ride to a remote village on the Burma border to visit a missionary medical doctor. More amazing comments from Lorie regarding the work being done in primitive areas by keen, caring people.

Finally I was able to take my daughter to Dara to meet my students. I don't know who enjoyed it more. The girls were so eager to ask Lorie questions that their English suddenly improved! No one wanted to quit and they followed Lorie around the campus as she visited different classes. It didn't take her long to discover why I was so happy working with these beautiful young Thai girls.

We spent our final days together talking about her work at the University, how her dissertation was coming, the lectures she was giving as a TA. It seems she was a happy lecturer as she spoke enthusiastically about her classes. I knew she must enjoy teaching for she had recently received an award as the outstanding TA in her department. I reminded her of the conversation we had had when she decided to go on for a PhD. At that time I asked, "What do you plan to do with a Doctor's degree. Would you teach?" Without hesitation she replied, "Oh, **no**. I'll never be a teacher." This stunned me and hurt a bit as she had grown up in a home with both parents in the teaching profession. What kind of an impression had we made on her? I also wondered if it reflected on her relationship with her father. And now, another comparison.

Lee was often voted the favorite teacher by his high school students. Like father, like daughter!

When Lorie began organizing her clothes and Thai treasures for her return trip to California, she asked if she could have the bouquet of opium poppy pods that I had in a pretty celadon vase. I assured her that the custom officials would not look lightly on these, even if they were dried.

A different girl left Thailand. It was good. Everything was not said, but I knew we'd talk about it in the future at the right time. She made the round of goodbyes to her new friends with sincere promises of a return visit. Lorie and I agreed that the country and people of Thailand were just the best. As she headed for her plane in Bangkok, I could hear her singing softly to our favorite San Francisco song, "I left my heart in Chiang Mai, Thailand"

A few days later Lorie phoned to say she was home safely. "I'm so glad I didn't put the poppies in my suitcase!" she said. "When I went through customs they asked where I'd been and when I told them, the Golden Triangle, the Burma border, etc., they said, 'Open your suitcase!' You remember the last thing I packed and laid on top of my clothes, were the folders of all the pictures we'd taken. Well, these agents began looking at them, asked who you were and what you were doing in Thailand. When I told them you were a teacher and when they saw all the interesting things we'd done, they exclaimed over the pictures, shut the suitcase, and said what a lucky person I was. You were right again, Mom!" As we hung up I thought, "Yes, Moms do come in handy at times."

VACATION THAI STYLE

Something was up! I sensed excitement in the air as soon as I walked through the English Department door. Before I had taken two steps into the room Acharn Perla and Acharn Patcheree jumped out of their chairs and rushed toward me, both talking at once. When they finally realized I could not understand a thing they said, they both collapsed into uncontrollable laughter. Acharn Naraporn, realizing that these young teachers were helpless to continue, took over. She explained that the school had just announced they were offering to pay each teacher half the expenses of a vacation trip to Southern Thailand during the semester break.

"You've got to come with us," they exclaimed. "You've never been to Southern Thailand and Phuket is the best place to go. You must see it before you leave for the states next month. It will be such fun if we go together. We'll be on the Malaysian border where you can buy all sorts of things and everything is very cheap!"

When they had finished their detailed account of the trip and I was finally given all the information, it did seem like a good idea.

Four teachers from the English Department and Acharn Jackie marched over to the school office and signed up.

Why was everyone so excited about Phuket? I hurried home after school to do my research and found that it was an island off the southwest coast of Thailand not far from the Malaysian border. My Thai book said it was the country's leading producer of tin and one of its most attractive seaside resorts with gypsy fishing boats and beaches covered with exotic shells. Now I was really interested! They described the oldest luxury air-conditioned hotel on the island, the Tavaorn, which sounded exciting. I became even more enthusiastic when I read about the fabulous restaurants specializing in Indian Ocean lobster and other seafood.

I prepared for this trip by reminding myself that I was traveling "Thai style", not farang style. The first indication of the difference was when I was told to be at the station at 2 p.m. to catch the train for Bangkok. When I normally went to Bangkok I took the 5 p.m. non-stop train and traveled "Second Class Air." This meant I was in a clean, air-conditioned train with reserved, comfortable, cushioned seats which became bunks at night so I could sleep my way south. It was time I learned to travel like the others, so I eagerly climbed aboard the 2 p.m. train with the eighty teachers from Dara and found a seat with my friends on a wooden bench with a straight back and no padding.

Since the train was made up in Chiang Mai, it was not crowded and we sat comfortably with only two or three people per bench. Not so bad! I had learned back home to call this a "milk train" as I knew it would stop in every town we passed. However, the teachers described it as the "ice cream train" but could not explain why.

Yes, we did stop in every town and soon all the cars were crowded to overflowing. When the benches were packed with six people, the aisles filled and I counted at least twenty sitting or standing in the vestibule between cars. One young girl was actually sitting on the steps of the train, with no door to protect her, and I worried lest she fall asleep and end up on the tracks. Since this was the hot season within a very short time all traces of my last minute shower had disappeared. Yet I was wet.

All the open windows were very handy for the vendors who at every stop overwhelmed us with offers of fish, chicken, rice, soup, drinks, fruits, and even orchids! This continued at every station throughout the night, accentuated by loud shouts to make sure those who were sleeping knew there was something to be bought. Two young Thai girls, who had squeezed in between us, weren't a bit shy and one found my shoulder a convenient place for a nap. So, I ached from not moving and the vendor's shouts made sure if I dropped into a doze it wasn't for long. This was the easiest part of our trip for we were on the train for **only** sixteen hours.

We had been warned to use the lavatory before reaching Bangkok as there would be no time to stop before boarding our bus to complete our trip south. I assure you that using the squat toilets on a crowded, moving train was not the easiest or pleasantest thing to do!

What a relief to finally get out and be able to stretch our legs running the block to catch the bus. The big yellow vehicle did seem a bit cleaner than the train but possibly more crowded for we were assigned three to a seat with our knees touching the seat back in front. Everyone seemed to know that when you traveled like this, you first pulled the seat cushion out from the bus's side so there was a five-inch gap, which allowed the cushion to jut into the aisle for the third person to sit on. I was assigned a "middle" seat between Acharn Naraporn, who was a rather large woman, and a young Thai teacher who spoke no English.

At no time during the trip did both of my shoulders ever touch the back of the seat at the same time as we sat sandwich-style, alternating right and left shoulders every hour or so. This second segment of our journey took seventeen hours with the bus making three short stops for meals.

Traveling "Thai Style"

Traveling through the South of Thailand was like being in a different world. Instead of the familiar brilliant green rice paddies of Northern Thailand, we saw shady plantations of rubber trees. There were miles and miles of coconut, pineapple, and sugar cane and instead of the familiar orange sloping roof of a Buddhist temple there was the gilded dome of a Muslim mosque.

Everyone was relieved to straggle off the bus at 10 p.m. as the driver encouraged us to walk across the famous Sarasin Bridge onto Phuket Island. To me the bridge showed no signs of being special but I was assured this was the only correct way to arrive on Phuket. This meant our long trip on the bus was about to come to an end. As near as I could tell, we had traveled about 2,300 kilometers (1,430 miles) in thirty-three hours and covered most of the length of Thailand.

Another hour of riding and close to midnight we finally reached our hotel. It was a weary group that gathered in the lobby to receive keys and be assigned rooms. The "leader" delegated three people to each room but when she tried to split up the five members of the English Department there were loud protests. "We have to stay with Acharn Jackie!" they announced. Without a fuss we were given a key and the five of us headed for our room; a room with twin beds. No problem! The two beds were quickly pushed together so we could sleep crosswise and I was graciously offered the coveted middle space.

On our first day we were driven to those marvelous beaches I had read about. They were superb. The sand was white and soft. The sea shells, abundant and unbroken, were unlike any I had found on my California coast. These were colorful gold and orange with twists, curls and warty bumps. It was like being on a treasure hunt and stumbling over all the treasure.

The weather was warm and balmy, perfect for swimming. Where were the swimming suits? I had dutifully left mine in the bottom of my bag when I was informed that no female Thai teacher would be seen on a public beach in such a state of undress. A few brave souls wearing long shorts did take off their shoes to wade in the surf but I just had to watch.

What I found surprising and appreciated most was the lack of hotels along these spectacular beaches. One could drive or walk for miles and see nothing manmade but old wooden fishing boats, painted with bright floral designs. It was truly an idyllic setting and I could not bear to stay on shore with this unbelievably beautiful sea in front of me. Luckily I found a handsome young man standing next to one of the "gypsy" boats and asked him if he would take us out onto the water. He agreed, so the English Department clambered aboard and he skillfully rowed us out of the bay to the edge of the reef. Suddenly and silently he slipped over the side and down into the depths. We were all amazed and delighted when a magnificent piece of lavender coral, resembling a bouquet of tiny flowers, appeared, followed a few seconds later by our guide. Graciously he presented me with one of the most exquisite floral arrangements I've ever received!

I was still having difficulty understanding the rapid Thai spoken by the teachers, so in the ensuing days, I just watched and followed wherever they went. I hesitated to keep asking where we were going and what we were doing. This was their vacation and they didn't need to spend all of it translating for me. In a way, it was a pleasant, relaxing time, as I just tagged along following the crowd.

My watch said three a.m. and I was a bit disconcerted to be awakened while it was still dark. The teachers saw my puzzled look but insisted I get up and dress. Blindly I did as I was told and soon found myself on a bus headed up the coast. It was still dark when we parked at a dock and I stumbled after the group onto an old, dilapidated fishing boat tied to a pier. As soon as we were all aboard, we pulled away from shore and headed east into the Gulf of Thailand. Within a few minutes we were treated to a spectacular view of the sun breaking through a thin layer of clouds and rising over the sea. The dark blue water of the Gulf turned to soft rose and pink, smooth and still as a sea of rose petals—a sight well worth the three a.m. wake-up call.

I soon realized this was Phangnga Bay, another of Thailand's beauty spots. Through the morning mist we saw ahead of us the ghostly shapes of islands sticking straight up out of the water with no shore at all. The Thai have given these islands names after the shape of their silhouettes, such as Koh Ma Chu or "Puppy Island." We headed toward the base of a mountain and sailed into a cavern containing primitive paintings of animals and humans.

Our lunch stop was at a small restaurant on a large rock where a whole fishing village existed on stilts over the water. Old women under big black hats paddled their narrow boats between the houses selling bananas and papaya while men sat on the decks above mending their nets.

I didn't need to be told about the next stop for it was easy to recognize the island location of the James Bond movie, "Man With the Golden Gun." Our boat plowed ahead and just as we seemed to face certain disaster, we slipped into the barely discernible, overgrown entrance to a cave. We passed under giant stalactites and avoided the rocks that protruded from the water in our path. What an amazing place! No wonder they chose it for 007.

All during this trip I was being a good farang and eating the food the other teachers ordered, in an area that had the best sea food in the country. I think the most I ever paid for my share of a meal was 20 baht or about 87 cents, for it just didn't seem right to order lobster, prawns or crab for 70 or 80 baht. I also had to be careful about "treating" too often and appearing like a boastful American. I had certainly enjoyed most of the Thai food that I had eaten in the north, but now the steady diet of rice and noodles was getting to be a bit much. I dreamed of a slice of bread or a piece of cheese. Fortunately I had brought my own instant coffee as all the coffee ordered in Thailand already had sugar added and sometimes even cream—a disaster for a black coffee drinker like me. At least I was able to buy fresh fruit along the way so I survived the trip but would turn green thereafter if anyone even suggested fried rice for breakfast.

When we arrived at Haadyai on the Malaysia border, I finally discovered the main reason for the trip. It was **not** to go sight-seeing, but to shop. This town was a mecca for cheap electrical appliances and basic food stuffs. About one-third of the group bought either a radio or hi-fi set and all the teachers bought boxes of apples, instant cream, and coffee. At least six teachers bought three-foot long stuffed animals and Acharn Naraporn bought her niece a talking doll in a box 2 1/2 feet long.

The last day we were up at 3:30 a.m. as the vacation tour included several stops on the return to Bangkok before connecting with the 7:30 p.m. train back to Chiang Mai. Now just let your imagination wander back to the bus which is already crowded, and see me in the middle seat again, between one teacher holding a doll box on her lap and another holding a large hi-fi. The aisles that were initially full now included all the new purchases and were completely jammed which made it impossible for anyone sitting to try to stand, even if they, like me, had swollen feet and needed to get the circulation back.

The return trip was otherwise uneventful except for a flat tire and the driver being arrested for not stopping at a check point. This meant we had to retreat fifteen miles for him to pay a fine so now we were behind schedule. He drove the last three hours at 75 miles per hour, the bus lurching and bounding over the rough road and the horn honking the whole time. We arrived at the station in Bangkok with 25 minutes to spare.

I said goodbye to my Dara friends here since I was to stay in Bangkok to visit with Ruth and Bill for a few days. As I curled up that night in a single bed, all by myself, I reflected on this final Thai adventure. I realized that while I had made many Thai friends during my two-year stay, and observed their life and culture, before now I had not really experienced it myself. How grateful I was to end my two-year stay with a "Thai-style vacation." And sleeping five people on twin beds will be one of my fondest memories.

EXODUS

Saturday, June 2nd, 1984
Bangkok
Last day in Thailand

D ear Family,

When I write my book about my Thai Experience, I think the best chapter will be about my Exodus! After I arrived at the Guest House in Bangkok this morning, having taken the night train from Chiang Mai, the first thing I had to do was unpack all my suitcases and air my semi-damp clothes.

The weather was unbearably hot that last week in Chiang Mai necessitating my taking three or four showers each day. Unfortunately the hot weather also resulted in low water pressure so I had to carry buckets of water from downstairs up to my apartment. In addition we had no electricity which meant no overhead fan. As I could neither iron, dry my clothes nor use my curling iron to tame my unruly hair, you can imagine I did not leave Chiang Mai in the best shape.

But—it really didn't bother me as I felt it was a fitting end to my Thai Experience—Mai Pen Rai!!

Now I have a day to relax before my 23-hour flight back to the states. I shall have dinner tonight with Ruth and Bill who took me to the refugee camps when I first arrived here. I was so impressed with the work they were doing at that time, but now, two years later, I must carry a sad letter back to the States, addressed to their director at the United Nations High Commission on Refugees. Ruth and Bill are recommending that they close down the repatriation program for refugees because of so many problems. It is sad to think we cannot help these people who had to flee their homeland because they worked for our government during the Vietnam/Cambodian wars.

My last week in Chiang Mai was hectic but advance planning helped a lot. Several dates were added to my already full schedule.

I had dinner Tuesday evening with twenty friends at the home of Acharn Loar. You may remember my telling you about the Christmas party I attended in her home given for the teachers from her husband's school. Well, this time we sat on the floor eating fish, crab, and Thai food while we watched "Chann", the movie starring Acharn Loar and her father. Acharn was only five years old in 1927 when Cecil B. DeMille came to Chiang Mai and made this famous movie about elephants in Northern Thailand. Since Acharn's father was the best elephant trainer in the country he was chosen as the star and Acharn played the part of his daughter in the film. "Chann" was nominated for an Academy Award that year. Evidently the film was recently discovered in some archives in California and sent to Thailand where it was reissued. Acharn Loar had just returned from appearances in Bangkok and I was thrilled when she gave me a video of it to bring home so I can share it with you.

Wednesday morning I had breakfast with my neighbor, Joan, and we had time for a good long talk. I loved hearing about her singing career which included starring on Broadway with Enzio Pinza in "South Pacific." She has been the King's favorite singer since her arrival in Thailand and is often called to Bangkok to sing for him at special celebrations. When she married Allen she gave up her professional career to become a missionary and they now have a Thai theatrical group that travels around the country performing plays with a Christian message. Joan presented me with a five-candle brass candelabra which I shall cherish.

The Dara faculty had a "tea" for me with food and speeches and gave me a lovely engraved lacquerware plate. Then my office staff brought dinner to my house. We ate on the floor of my porch by candlelight (remember, **no** electricity!). I had a rather large collection of Thai treasures, still in one piece after the bombing, that I was unable to take home with me. There were Thai pillows, little tables, a few celadon dishes, plants, and assorted items including my vase containing the dried opium poppies. I chose not to try to get through customs with this bouquet! We started with Acharn Naraporn since she was head of the English Department and had a hilarious time as each took turns choosing an item until all were gone. A happy group of teachers trudged down the stairs after our party, their arms loaded with my leftovers.

On Thursday, Tony Teak and his sister took me to lunch. You all met Tony on your visits here for he and his sister own the Tony Teak shop on Thai Phae Road where I did much of my shopping. They gave me a beautiful cloth shoulder bag to go with the elegant Thai jacket they had made for me some months before.

At 6 o'clock that night I was picked up and taken to a party given for me by Ranoo. There I found twenty of my favorite people in Chiang Mai. These included friends from New Zealand, Australia, India, Thailand, and the States. Ranoo greeted us on her veranda in an exquisite long red and white gown. She really is one of the most beautiful women I know, with shoulder-length black hair hanging in soft curls around her face. She and I are the same age and lost our husbands two months apart, so we had shared our experiences many times over lunch during the past two years. Auntie Vi, who raised Ranoo, looked regal in a long violet dress adorned with her elegant family jewels. She is another beautiful lady whose father was a Scotsman and early director of the teak dealing Borneo Company, and her mother a famous Chiang Mai princess.

The table was filled with a wide assortment of delicious Thai dishes, each one beautifully decorated. We even had a glass of wine before we ate—an unusual treat in Thailand.

I was glad they had invited Pakdee, the minister of the Presbyterian church in Chiang Mai. This is the church you all attended when you visited me. He had brought his guitar and we sang Thai songs, American songs, and Australian songs. We danced as we sang and then they made me dance "Thai style." I'm sure I looked like a clod but how could I refuse? We had lots of laughs over my awkward attempt.

Jackie, Auntie Vi and Ranoo

It was a rare evening with choice people in an elegant home. It meant so much to have my last dinner party given for me by Thai friends. On the way home, Ruth said that she'd never seen a party like it given for any missionary who had been here for even 26 years. This really thrilled me and inwardly I whispered, "Mission accomplished." All the special events of the past week had been with Thai friends.

Friday morning Acharn Rojana picked me up at 7 a.m. on her

motorcycle to take me for my final visit to Dara. We drove through drizzling rain and darted around heavy morning traffic arriving in time to see and hear the girls sing the National Anthem and the King's Song. TEARS! The memory of those lovely young people, standing at attention throughout the campus in their red and white uniforms will remain with me forever.

Can you believe another party? This one was given by a different group of teachers in their office at 8:05 a.m.—the only time I was free—with a cake and sweet punch. More gifts—a lovely silver bracelet and necklace. It was hard to tear myself away from these dear friends but I had one more stop to make. Ruth had invited me for my final lunch in Chiang Mai.

After that I returned home where I frantically tried to dry some clothes in my little gas oven. I stopped after scorching several things and instead stuffed everything damp into plastic bags. I finished packing with Jon Som, my helper, in a continuous state of tears. I finally chose a reasonably decent looking skirt and blouse without too many wrinkles to wear to the station. I knew the tradition of everyone coming to see you off when you left the country and wished I could look a bit more glamorous.

It was late afternoon and the Thai-style goodbye at the station was overwhelming. There were fifty to sixty Dara students, at least thirty Dara teachers and about fifty friends. Mr. Viechai who owns the big camera shop in town and who had already given me two of his famous Wat mural photographs, came early to take pictures. After shooting a roll of film he put it into my hands as the train pulled away.

When the film is developed you will see pictures of the elaborate leis given to me by the Dara School Manager—on a gold tray— and one by Uncle Angus, Auntie Vi's brother. In addition I was given six bouquets of roses and one of carnations. The night before at the dinner party, Pakdee had given me a large wicker basket and at the time I had wondered how I could possibly carry it home with me but, it certainly came in handy now.

It was a challenge to wear those two elaborate leis, hold seven bouquets of flowers, try to accept a gift and wai at the same time.

A loving Thai farewell

It was hard to greet everyone, so I simply stood next to the train and they came to me, making little speeches. I held the tears back until Donna and the group started singing, "Bless be the tie that binds!" A whistle blew. Time to go. Pakdee jumped on the train with me, hurriedly placed all the presents and flowers on my seat and left. Tears blurred my view of waving friends as we chugged out of the station.

Fortunately two acquaintances rode with me to Bangkok so we spent some time sorting things out. We opened the gifts and found boxes for the flowers. Many did not survive overnight but I now have three bouquets of roses here in my room at the Bangkok Christian Guest House.

Later—I'm now at the Don Muang Airport, first in line for Thai International Flight # 740. Next stop—USA! I had a delicious dinner last night at an Indian restaurant with Ruth and Bill, then over to the Oriental Hotel for dessert. We sat outdoors at a table by the river so we could enjoy the interesting night boat traffic—under a new moon. Significant?

I'm excited about about my future. Something new for me?

The last chapter of my "Thai Pilgrimage" has ended. It was a great adventure. I'm feeling high. The past two years simply flew by. I came—I saw—I felt—I experienced. So much happened. What did it all mean? I can't wait to get into my seat on the plane, sit quietly, and have time to reflect.

Much love,
Acharn Jackie

FLYING INTO A NEW DAY

The cabin of the airplane is dark and quiet. A few reading lights are still on. Dinner has been served and the movie is over. Flight attendants hide behind their curtains and I can hear them talking softly as we head out across the dark Pacific. The sliver of new moon in the distance reminds me of my thoughts last evening. A new moon—a new life for me? I came to Asia on a pilgrimage, to "restore my soul." Had it happened? The dark and the quiet suit my searching mind.

I know I am different from that person who arrived in a raging storm two years ago. But, what is different? I know I feel calmer and less anxious.

I had much time there to be alone, time to read, time to just be quiet and I now realize that I never felt "lonely" but enjoyed being by myself. Living in a mission compound where the gates were locked at dusk for security, I rarely went out in the evening and grew to cherish those times when I could shut my door and retreat into my room away from the world. Back home this would be impossible with phones to ring, a house full of college students, TV going, and a car handy at all times. It had turned out to be a real plus **not** having a telephone, a TV, or a car.

Time to read was also a luxury. Not just a few minutes squeezed in when I went to bed at night too tired to appreciate a good story, but time to savor. American consulate friends shared the latest pocket books from the States, but friends in the Mission community shared favorite books from their seminary studies or favorite authors who challenged us to think about the world, our own lives, and our place in society.

I'm sure that living in a Buddhist culture also had a great impact on me. The majority of teachers at Dara were Buddhists and I became a recipient of their Buddhist practices. Through their kindness I found my desk dusted or washed each morning when I arrived at my office. Flowers were regularly in place and even mentioning that I liked or admired something made it mine. Their thoughtfulness and desire to "do for others" without thanks or recognition was a good lesson.

In an office of seven adults, the conversation was always low keyed, the walking slow. I **never** saw teachers run or even walk fast on campus. Everything about them was calming and it all helped slow me down. Often I had compared or wondered about the difference between a "good Christian" and a "good Buddhist." But I could find little difference. Now the challenge will be to carry this Buddhist pace back to the States with me.

Before I left home two years ago I gave my favorite prayer book, *A Diary of Private Prayer,* by John Baillie, to several friends and family. We all pledged to read the daily selections each morning and evening and this was my tie across the miles. I also subscribed to my favorite contemplative journal and in this Buddhist setting, it was easy to take time each morning to read these inspirational publications. Buddhist monks passing my window were a constant reminder of their meditation practices and this encouraged me with mine.

Then there were all the trips I took to experience and view the real side of life in this underdeveloped country. It was sad to view the crippled patients at McKean undergoing treatment for leprosy, but encouraging to learn about the progress being made with this disease.

I saw and heard many distressing things involving the tribal people of the northern Thai mountains. There was the ill treatment by local police, the fighting on the Burma border, the poverty and the hunger. But I also remember going with Dr. Sukitt and his medical team to "minister unto the least of these." Those trips with missionaries over rugged back mountain roads—taking blankets, rice, and malaria pills and introducing new skills to these impoverished people to help improve their standard of living, were an inspiration.

Will I ever forget the refugee camps—the hopelessness of those displaced persons?

What did it all mean? Was I just an interested "tourist observer?" No, I think my soul was truly touched by the injustices I saw. I can never be the same. Now I wonder how this will affect my life back home.

I was blessed to meet so many fascinating people from around the world who work in that troubled area helping others. How could they help but influence me with their sense of dedication. And they were such joyful people!

But now I am overwhelmed thinking of my Thai friends. And I really can call them FRIENDS. They taught me so much. They loved unconditionally. They accepted this hyper, energy-driven teacher and inspired me to be like them.

Yes, I have changed. My soul has been not only restored but challenged, and I also understand that my prilgrimage has not been in vain. It allowed me to reach an understanding of the wife I was and the reasons for my husband's death.

Where is all that guilt I carried to Thailand with me? I realize I have scarcely thought about it in recent months. Maybe it was having enough quiet time away from the busy-ness of America to review Lee's life.

Maybe those things I thought about: the lack of affection and recognition, the reading problems, the amount of chemicals he poured into his body over the years and the constant nagging pain that he endured. None of these was my fault. Oh, I know I'm not blameless but I also know that I did the best I could at that time. If only we had a second chance!

One of the greatest lessons I have learned is that, however much I love them, I cannot live other people's lives for them. Happiness and peace can only come from within.

Of course I shall never feel completely free of the grief, but now I have forgiven myself.

Before I tuck the pillow behind my head for sleep, I look out the window and see a glow in the sky as we head East. A new day has begun.